COLLEGE ADMISSIONS

FOR THE 21ST CENTURY

COLLEGE ADMISSIONS FOR THE 21ST CENTURY

Robert J. Sternberg

HARVARD UNIVERSITY PRESS
Cambridge, Massachusetts & London, England
2010

To Henry Chauncey, Jr.

Library of Congress Cataloging-in-Publication Data

Sternberg, Robert J.
College admissions for the 21st century / Robert J. Sternberg.
  p. cm.
Includes bibliographical references and index.
ISBN 978-0-674-04823-2 (cloth : alk. paper)
1. Universities and colleges—United States—Admission.   2. Education, Higher—
Standards—United States.   3. Educational equalization—United States.   I. Title.
LB2351.2.S74 2010
378.1′61—dc22   2010011512

CONTENTS

PREFACE

I entered into the admissions business as a sophomore in college. I was interested in how my college, Yale, could improve its admissions procedures. I had the audacity to write to Henry (Sam) Chauncey, Jr., dean of undergraduate admissions and financial aid policy, and son of the president of the Educational Testing Service, asking him whether he would be interested in creating a job for me in the Yale undergraduate admissions office. This brazen approach had worked for me before, having yielded summer jobs for me at two companies that created psychological tests, The Psychological Corporation (then in New York City) and the Educational Testing Service (in Princeton, New Jersey). I had the first of these jobs during two high-school summers, and the second when I started college.

Chauncey replied and scheduled an interview. He must have been at least somewhat impressed, because he hired me. I am glad he did, because I learned a lot and moreover because to this day he remains a lifelong friend.

For two and a half years I worked part-time in admissions and then, after graduating early, I became a special assistant to the dean of undergraduate admissions, who at the time was a man named John Muyskens. I spent a semester doing what admissions officers do, as well as researching undergraduate admissions. Those were heady times during the early 1970s, when we all believed that we could make the world a better place if only we admitted the "right" students to Yale.

I decided that, in order to pursue my interests properly, I would need a PhD, so after that one semester I headed to Stanford as a PhD student in psychology. There I would begin what has become a lifelong program of research into the nature of human abilities, their antecedents, and their consequences. One of my mentors, Lee Cronbach, told me that the field of human intelligence was pretty much dead. But I have done what I can to revive it over more than thirty years of teaching and research, during which my interest in admissions has never wavered.

Three years after entering Stanford, I received my PhD and headed back to Yale as an assistant professor. I was determined to change the way people thought about abilities, and the way such abilities were tested and developed. I suppose that, in the ideal world, I would be writing in this preface about my enormous successes. I've had some: along the way I have picked up numerous awards and eleven honorary doctorates. But I have had little or no success in changing the way this nation tests for or develops human abilities.

The traditional, narrow approach to admissions testing reminds me of an experience I had last summer, while traveling with my wife. She and I sat in a restaurant with a spectacular view of an enormous waterwheel that was spinning and churning water as it had been for scores of years. The wheel looked perhaps a bit worse for wear, but it continued to do, after all the years, the job it was constructed to do. It was offered by the town as a historical landmark—one that tourists like us could enjoy.

The standardized tests we use today are roughly as old in their conception as that waterwheel is in its execution. But these tests are not treated merely as items of historical interest; instead they play a central part in determining which students will make it into which colleges. Imagine what the world would be like today if medical, telecommunications, computing, or other technologies were stuck at the beginning of the twentieth century. Many diseases that are now curable or at least treatable would kill people who now can stay alive. People would be writing all their correspondence with a fountain pen and ink, or with clunky typewriters, instead of with a computer. Overseas telephone calls would still be an expensive novelty. Today's standardized tests, metaphorically speaking, are those historical novelties.

That said, the message of this book is not that the standardized tests we use today are horrible and evil, and that the world would be a better place if they were to disappear overnight. On the contrary, such tests, like every other measure used in college admissions, have both strengths and weaknesses. For many individuals and groups, they are reasonable although not excellent predictors of academic success in college. They tell something about a student's academic potential. A student with SAT scores in the low 300s is less likely, on average, to succeed academically in a highly selective college than a student with scores in the high 600s.

At the same time, scores can be raised or lowered by many extenuating circumstances that the scores, by their very nature, cannot take into account—differences in education, first language, home environment, conditions of testing, and so forth. My argument is not that tests are intrinsically bad, but rather that the information they give is incomplete—they are not enough. We can do better by devising new assessments that supplement the old ones and that more comprehensively reflect the psychology of today, not just of yesterday.

Every time one writes a book, one hopes to change the world. If the past is the best predictor of the future, I will not succeed with this book. But then, if the future were no different from the past, we would still be traveling by horse and buggy. So this book represents my hope that it is possible for our society to change course and recognize that our traditional way of doing things with regard to admissions, instruction, and assessment is less than optimal and has been for quite a long time. We need to move beyond our horse and buggy mentality in educational instruction and assessment, and to admit students to college not just on the basis of their academic skills with a few other extras thrown in, but rather on the basis of a student's overall potential to make a positive difference to the world.

We can do a much better job of college admissions, as well as instruction and assessment, if we think about student abilities in a broader way than we have—in particular, by valuing, assessing, and teaching for analytical, creative, practical, and wisdom-based skills as well as for memory. The book is divided into seven chapters that explain in detail the problem and possible solutions. In Chapter 1, I introduce basic ideas about college admissions and testing. I also review some of the basic history but do not try to mimic the comprehensive overviews that others have written. In Chapter 2, I discuss the basic elements of the college admissions process, as well as their strengths and weaknesses. In Chapter 3, I discuss alternative admissions practices. In Chapter 4, I present a new way of looking at the abilities needed for college success. In Chapter 5, I discuss how one can assess talents that typically remain hidden. In Chapter 6, I discuss teaching in ways that promote intelligence, creativity, and wisdom. I argue that although admissions and instruction are usually seen as separate issues in colleges and universities, this separation is a mistake. Students should be admitted in ways that reflect the way teaching is done, and teaching should also reflect these new admissions practices. In Chapter 7, I close by exploring the implications of the arguments in the book.

I would like to acknowledge those who have made an extraordinary difference to this book. Sam Chauncey provided me with the opportunity, during my college days, to become involved in admissions, and I thank him for that and for remaining a lifelong friend. My undergraduate and graduate advisers, Endel Tulving at Yale and Gordon Bower at Stanford, supported my research interests in abilities, even though those interests were quite different from theirs. During my career as a faculty member at Yale, the late Wendell Garner supported me even though I worked in a very nontraditional area of psychology. And at Tufts, President Lawrence Bacow and Provost Jamshed Bharucha have created an atmosphere of positive transformation and leadership development. Dean of Admissions Lee Coffin, together with the Tufts undergraduate admissions staff, creatively and effectively implemented the Kaleidoscope Project in a way I suspect few if any other admissions offices could match. The data analyses for the Kaleidoscope Project discussed in the book were done primarily by Christina Rhee Bonney, Liane Gabora, and Tzur Karelitz, and the entire undergraduate admissions office at Tufts made a somewhat vague idea an operational reality.

My colleagues on the Tufts faculty and in the administration have been unwavering in their efforts to create the best education a college student could hope for. I especially thank Linda Jarvin, formerly deputy director of the PACE Center at Tufts, for her collaboration in this work. All of the collaborators in the Rainbow and Kaleidoscope Projects have provided enormous assistance, and I thank especially Elena Grigorenko and Steven Stemler, who collaborated in all phases of the Rainbow Project. I also thank Provost Jamshed Bharucha, Joshua Butts, Anne Fishman, Karin Sternberg, and Kim Thurler for their comments on an earlier version of this manuscript. Dean of Admissions Lee Coffin did an especially close reading of an early version and pointed out many details in need of modification; I am especially grateful to him for the substantial time he invested and for the many excellent points he raised. Two anonymous reviewers also provided helpful comments. Elizabeth Knoll of Harvard University Press has been a wonderful editor throughout the development of this book. Most of all, my wife, Karin Sternberg, has been a source of ideas and inspiration for much of the work I have described.

Thanks go as well to the study participants and other young people whose experiences are detailed here; I have changed all such names to protect their privacy.

I would like to add special thanks to five people without whose influence in my early life this book would not have been possible. The late Virginia Alexa, my fourth-grade teacher, saved me from the self-defeating, self-fulfilling prophecies that accompanied my then-low IQ test scores. By giving me a chance, she changed the trajectory of my life from one that was slowly descending to one that could ascend and bring me to where I am today. The late William Adams, my seventh-grade science teacher, stood up for me when I got into trouble giving IQ tests to some of my seventh-grade classmates. When I was being threatened with disciplinary action, he was a lifeboat that kept me on track. He also enabled me to maintain my interest in psychology in general, and intelligence in particular. Carol Stewart, my tenth-grade biology teacher, encouraged my interest in assessment, and even allowed me to compare the learning of students in her class to that of students in a more traditional biology class, a risk on her part that many other teachers never would have taken. Irwin Genzer, my eleventh-grade physics teacher, allowed me to do a physics project that involved creating a physics aptitude test, even though the project had a lot to do with psychology and much less to do with physics. Finally, I would like to thank my freshman-year psychology professor, the late Robert G. Crowder, who, despite giving me an ignoble C in introductory psychology, supported me as an upper-level student in psychology, when I applied to Yale for an assistant professorship, and when I came up for tenure at Yale. Many of us forget the huge difference our early teachers make to who we become in later life. Without these teachers and others too many to name, this book never would have been written.

The views expressed in this book are my own. They do not represent the views either of Tufts University or of any particular individuals who have worked at Tufts, other than myself. My work on admissions has been funded at various times by diverse organizations, most notably the Institute for Educational Sciences of the U.S. Department of Education, the College Board, the Spencer Foundation, the National Science Foundation, the James S. McDonnell Foundation, the U.S. Army Research Institute, and private donors to Tufts University. The views expressed here do not represent the views of any individuals in these organizations nor of the organizations as a whole. Thus I take full and exclusive responsibility for any ideas to which you may object that you encounter in this book.

COLLEGE ADMISSIONS AND TESTING

Waiting list. That was the long-awaited outcome of my application to Yale. It was better than the outcome at Harvard, which was a rejection, and not as good as the outcome at Princeton, which was an acceptance. But I wanted to go to Yale.

I was to have one opportunity that few applicants would ever get. I was eventually admitted to Yale off the waiting list, and went there, later to graduate summa cum laude, Phi Beta Kappa. The opportunity I had was to find out why I was wait-listed. Right after graduation, I was working as a special assistant to the dean of admissions at Yale. With the encouragement of some of my colleagues, I sneaked up into the dusty old attic where old admissions records were kept. I did not read my whole admissions file—I felt too guilty—but I did not feel guilty enough to pass up reading my Yale interview report.

I remembered well my interview visit to Yale. It was a disaster. It was pouring cats and dogs. I wanted to major in psychology and so visited the psychology department. They hooked me up with a postdoctoral fellow who was implanting electrodes in cats' brains. I was revolted. They had just painted the psychology department, and I got bright blue paint on my raincoat that never did come off. And my interview was worst of all. In the interview report, which I discovered up in the attic, the interviewer said I had a "flakey personality." And did Yale want a flakey personality? When I finally did get in, it was through the intervention of the admissions officer for my area, Bill Robinson, who saw something in me.

Great schools do not always produce flawless leaders. Harvard Business School produced Jeffrey Skilling, former CEO of Enron and convicted felon. Yale College, my own alma mater, produced George W. Bush, whose invasion of Iraq was based on intelligence that even he later admitted was faulty. Yale Law School produced Bill Clinton, whose inability to control his self-destructive tendencies resulted in an impeachment that severely undermined the legacy of his presidency. Dennis Kozlowski, who went to college at Seton Hall, a few miles away from where I was going to high school at the same time in New Jersey, was convicted of looting his company. When he was CEO, Tyco paid $1 million for his wife's fortieth birthday party. The party, billed as a shareholder meeting, featured a statue of Michelangelo's David urinating Stolichnaya vodka. Kozlowski also had Tyco pay for his $6,000 shower curtains.[1]

Such examples of flawed behavior by very successful college applicants, however, only imperfectly capture the problem of college admissions. At least as problematic are the many people who look as though they have great potential at age seventeen or eighteen but don't look so great twenty years later, along with the potentially great ones who get away. In talking to a high-level executive at a major investment bank, I mentioned our desire to enhance admissions at Tufts University. His response, based on his twenty-five years of experience on Wall Street, was that tests like the SAT and the ACT, as well as college grades, predicted quite well who would be good analysts. That is, they predicted the technical skills needed to evaluate various investments. What they did not predict as well was who would be able to take the next step—who would have the capacity to envision where various markets are going, to see larger trends, and to make decisions that went beyond individual stock or bond picks. Are great schools missing something in how they admit students and how they teach them?

All great schools seek students who will enhance the excellence and diversity of their classes. They want students who will shine in the classroom and then excel in later life, making the world a better place in which to live. Are we really doing the best we can, as a society, in selecting and developing the best generation of leaders? Do the current elements of a college application identify these traits and abilities in a maximally effective way? Or is there something lacking in what we are doing? That is, are we always going to be stuck with a few bad apples, no matter our methods, or is there something wrong with the way we pick and sort the apples in the field?

I believe that the problem is not just with a few bad apples, or with our sorting methods, but with society: at some level, we all contribute to it. Some parents push their kids relentlessly to get better scores on standardized tests, often paying obscene fees to tutors ($500 and more a session in some New York suburbs). College and university administrators contract with testing companies to use these standardized tests so that they can admit applicants they believe to be qualified—as well as, in some cases, to compete in *U.S. News* and other ratings sweepstakes. College and university faculty want students with high test scores who will do well on the professors' own tests. Students dutifully take the tests, and they or their parents pay for the tests that may get them into, or keep them out of, the colleges they dream of attending. The test companies continue to market roughly the same tests they have been selling for a century. And the government is blind to what seems to some to be the monopolistic hold that two test companies have on the college admissions market.

Here, as a teaser, are the six main claims of this book:

- Tests such as the SAT and the ACT are not "bad," but rather incomplete. They measure memory and analytical skills, which make up only a fraction of the skills that are important for college and life success.
- The solution to the incompleteness of such tests is not to replace them, but to supplement them or to have tests that measure not only what the traditional tests measure, but also other qualities.
- Other skills that are important to measure are creative skills, practical skills, and wisdom-based skills. To succeed in school and in life, one needs creative skills to generate new ideas, analytical skills to ascertain whether they are good ideas, practical skills to execute the ideas and to persuade others of their worth, and wisdom-based skills to ensure that the ideas help attain a common good, not just selfish gain.
- Using tests of these additional skills increases prediction of both academic attainment and meaningful participation in extracurricular and leadership activities in college.
- Using such tests simultaneously with standardized testing reduces, potentially substantially, ethnic-group differences in overall test performance.
- In the end, such enhanced admissions procedures benefit candidates for admission, the colleges to which they apply, and society at large.

Some, such as Frank Schmidt, John Hunter, and others, have suggested that we keep using conventional tests because they worked in the past and they work in the present.[2] I agree. They do work, at some level. They predict modestly to moderately many different kinds of skills, from getting A's in school to following complex regimens with prescription drugs. They also can help admissions officers sort out students who may not be able to do the academic work in a given college from those who are more likely to be able to do that work. The problem is that today, as in the past, their prediction is far from perfect. Remember, early medicine and early telephones worked too. They just did not work all that well. And the reason they developed rapidly and standardized testing has not is simple—competition.

When the telephone companies were deregulated and AT&T lost its monopoly, telephone technology and service began to expand at a fast clip. In the computer-related fields, competition meant that businesses like Control Data Corporation (CDC) that did not innovate died, while those businesses that did innovate, such as International Business Machines (IBM), survived and even thrived. Drug companies today compete for ever greater shares of markets. But two companies largely control the market for college admissions tests, with one substantially larger than the other and with each having areas of control rather tightly defined by region of the country. These companies would themselves benefit from increased competition, as does any company that wants to produce the best possible consumer products.

IMPROVING THE SYSTEM: VALUING ADDITIONAL SKILLS

Although the current system of admissions is good, it can be substantially better. We can do a much better job of college admissions, as well as instruction and assessment, if we think about student abilities in a broader way than we have—in particular, by valuing, assessing, and teaching for analytical, creative, practical, and wisdom-based skills as well as for memory-related ones. In particular, I propose that students should be admitted to college on the basis of their potential for future leadership and active citizenship, at whatever level of society (from the family, to the workplace and other communities, to the world), by taking into account, among other criteria, their having the academic knowledge and skills necessary for success in college work.

I define leadership here not in the sense of achieving a level of authority, but rather as making a positive, meaningful, and hopefully enduring difference to the world at some level. Many current admissions processes seek an understanding of a broad range of talents, but test scores and school grades, because they are quantified, may get proportionally more weight than they deserve in a holistic admissions process. Such tests are somewhat narrow in the spectrum of knowledge and skills they measure, and need supplementation by assessments that draw on broader theories of human abilities and competencies. Such broader tests would help to create systems of admissions that are more nearly equitable for the individuals applying to college, including those from diverse socioeconomic backgrounds who have hidden talents to offer, and would improve outcomes—both in terms of academic quality and diversity—for universities and society as well.

This broader vision of the ideal college student should also influence the education of these students. Although colleges often treat admissions and instruction or assessment as distinct and autonomous operations, they need to be coordinated so that instruction matches the abilities selected for in admissions. For example, if a college seeks creative students through its admissions program, then it must also help instructors teach in ways that encourage and value creative thinking, lest students find themselves in an environment incompatible with the very skills for which they were admitted.

WHY IS CHANGE NEEDED?

There is something lacking in the way college admissions are conducted. We are not admitting people as we ideally should and could, and the academic disciplines are not doing a perfect job of cultivating students' skills, including their ethical ones. It is not that we are doing a bad job; it is that we can do much better. Neither testing companies, nor admissions officers, nor any other group is entirely to blame. Rather our society, as a whole, has created a system of interlocking parts that do not work together as well as they could—and it will be hard to fix because so many people do not even recognize that there is a problem.

Kenneth Lay, who like Jeffrey Skilling was both a former CEO of Enron and a convicted felon, had earned a doctorate and was a professor of economics. Did academic knowledge save him from helping to destroy a company with thousands of employees and customers? Apparently not. Of course, there are many well-educated people who are wonderful citizens and great leaders. But to the extent they are either, it may be not because of their knowledge base, but rather because they understand what to do with it.

Until the 1960s, most students were admitted to selective colleges on the basis of their parents' social class. It was believed that one's social class would predict in great measure one's potential for future positive leadership.

In the 1960s, Inslee Clark, dean of admissions at Yale, and others involved in college admissions had a new vision—one of an elite chosen primarily on the basis of merit rather than largely on privilege. No longer would it be enough merely to come from an affluent family, or to have acquired an education at one of the elite private schools in the nation. Some great students might come from well-endowed families and elite private schools, but then, some might come from very poor families and public schools with few resources. So the colleges started giving test scores and grades more weight in their deliberations, and parental wealth and privilege less. The result was a new generation of leaders who were supposedly chosen on their merits rather than by the luck of the draw at birth.

Given the leaders we have—ones who led Lee Iacocca to write the book *Where Have All the Leaders Gone?*— we have to question whether something went wrong somewhere along the line.[3] Actually, several things went wrong, and these problems are still with us today.

We Need to Identify and Nurture Potential Leaders
The first problem was that test scores correlated highly, although not perfectly, with social class.[4] This correlation is not fixed;

rather, parents of children from upper socioeconomic classes inadvertently increase this correlation. They, unlike less well-off parents, can afford to spend substantial sums of money having their children tutored for the tests they will have to take, so that these students come to have an edge in the testing sweepstakes. It is understandable that well-off parents would pay for such tutoring: they are trying to do the best for their children. If only test scores well predicted future leadership, then we might be back to our hope that family legacy could predict who will make a positive difference to the world in the future. But they offer no magic numbers for predicting future leadership or anything else.

This problem is an example of what is sometimes known as a Matthew effect. The Matthew effect derives from a statement in the Bible: "For unto every one that hath shall be given, and he shall have abundance: but from him that hath not shall be taken away even that which he hath" (Matthew 25:29). In other words, the rich get richer, and the poor get poorer.

The late Robert Merton, a sociologist at Columbia University, applied this principle to scientists: those at well-known schools who already had a good reputation received more resources, whereas those at poorly known schools who had little reputation received less, resulting in the further derailment of their careers.[5] But the Matthew principle applies as well to college admissions. If your parents can send you to strong schools and pay for tutelage, they can help bring you to a position where you are more competitive for college admissions; if your parents cannot pay, it becomes increasingly difficult to gain access on the basis of traditional measures of merit. Good admissions officers will take these factors into account and consider access to resources when evaluating applications.

Why should a correlation of test scores with socioeconomic status even be a problem? After all, if students from higher socioeconomic strata are able to perform better in college, then why not simply let them in, that is, why not simply follow the college admissions tests, which would accurately predict their performance?

There is no simple answer to this question and the answers one provides are a matter of policy, not psychology. But I believe there are three reasons why the correlation is problematic. To understand these reasons fully, you will need to imagine a society that educates well those people with blue eyes but poorly educates people with brown eyes, having decided that eye color is a good measure of the educational and perhaps other resources to which a person is entitled. (In our society, of course, historically we have used gender and skin color, which are equally arbitrary.) When the children reach high school, society gives them a test. The blue-eyed children outscore the brown-eyed children by a large margin and then, because college admissions are largely determined by test scores, the blue-eyed children dominate the numbers in college.

The first reason I can think of for not settling for such an outcome is that if one makes decisions largely on test scores, as partial proxies for socioeconomic status (which itself may be a proxy for other things), then one reduces one's chances of creating a more equitable society. There will be those who will say that society has been fair, because it gave preference to those who deserved it. Unsurprisingly, many, but not all, who think that way will have blue eyes. Many of the brown-eyed adults may say that their children were never given a chance, but the brown-eyed adults will have less money and power in society, and will not be well heard. Moreover, some of those who do hear them will view their complaints as sour grapes. Without some kind of admissions program that looks for strengths in the brown-eyed children, the society will be stuck with a hereditary hierarchy that seems merit-based—at least to those with blue eyes, including educators, scientists, government officials, and others who are perfectly rational on many matters not pertaining to the continued social empowerment and well-being of themselves and their children.

The second reason is that the brown-eyed children may actually be better in some skill areas than the blue-eyed children. This superiority will probably not show up in assessments created by typical blue-eyed adults, who have come to view as valuable those skills in which they and their children excel. But without efforts to devise measures that may do justice to the full range of skills of all children, one may in effect create tests skewed to favor those with blue eyes. Moreover, the teachers, who are also primarily blue-eyed or at least trained by those with blue eyes, will value the same narrower range of skills. So they will construct assessments that match the college admissions test, in the same way that the college admissions test may well originally have been created to value what the blue-eyed teachers, or those teachers trained by those with blue eyes, value. The tests will seem fair because the system is created to value what it is that blue-eyed people, on average, are precieved to do well, but not what brown-eyed people, on average, are precieved to do well.

The third reason, already implied, is that the criterion may be as biased, in a sense, as the predictor. When people are hired for high-level jobs, employers often consider what college the student went to (for example, Harvard versus Stinky U), and what kinds of grades the student received. But schools and grades are a highly imperfect predictor of job performance. The recent debacle on Wall Street is an example. It was created largely by individuals with excellent grades at terrific business schools. It was their ascent into positions of great power that enabled them to bring down not only Wall Street, but much of the economic system of the United States and the world as well. Indeed, it is a testament to the system's inherent bias that, when some of the "blue eyes" were fired for extraordinarily incompetent performance, they received severance packages—and many still there are receiving bonuses—in excess of what many brown-eyed people will make over their entire lifetimes. Heads they win; tails, others lose.

It is important to note in this consideration that high-school grades have correlations with socioeconomic status that may be as great as or even greater than those of the standardized tests.[6] So ditching the tests in favor of considering only school grades might solve some problems, but not that of the correlation of academic performances with socioeconomic status. The correlation of socioeconomic status with high-school performance is not terribly surprising. Educated parents can help their high-school student children in ways that less educated parents cannot. In my own case, neither of my parents had graduated from high school. They could help me in school, but perhaps not in the same way as could the parents of some of my classmates, who held doctorate degrees.

We Need to Reward, and Teach, a Broader Range of Skills

The second problem is that the tests were narrow in their conception. In the early twentieth century, when the tests were first devised, perhaps the abstract, academic skills they measured served as a somewhat reasonable basis for distinguishing more able white males of privilege from less able ones. But by the early twenty-first century, the skill set one needs for success in college and life has substantially broadened. Academic knowledge alone will not get one through; the world simply changes too quickly. (More on this later.) For this reason, many colleges use holistic admissions practices that take into account credentials beyond just academic knowledge.

It is worth emphasizing that the system we have now was made to create equity, not to destroy it. In earlier times, the main way one got ahead was through family connections. Tests were designed to create an objective measure of potential that would move beyond family ties. The procedures may have made sense in the early twentieth century, when the only people taking the tests were the children of privilege, so one could distinguish better among them who had more potential. But as the range of students taking the tests has increased, and their backgrounds have become more diverse, what had worked in the early twentieth century simply no longer works as well. One can no longer assume that almost all the test takers have similar upbringings, backgrounds, and opportunities for schooling. New tests are needed to reflect this new reality. But none of the new tests in development has yet been widely accepted.

The third problem is that the tests transformed secondary schooling, and not necessarily for the better. Students have come to spend more and more time preparing for tests, and less and less time learning lessons that may be meaningful to them in later life. Education has come, in some measure, to be replaced by gamesmanship. Music, art, physical education, and even, in some schools, social studies and science have gone by the wayside if they are not formally tested by the states.

WHY TESTING HAS CHANGED SO LITTLE

How has the testing game come to take over not only schooling, but even much of society? The route to the "takeover" has been a series of unfortunate collateral consequences of testing that has entrenched it ever more firmly in society's psyche. The problems that have resulted have little to do with the way admissions officers think. Admissions officers are, for the most part, very skilled at what they do. Rather, the problem is a societal one, reflecting the way society in general reacts to decision-making practices regarding college.

Traditional Tests Seem Precise

Tests yield quantified, seemingly precise measures of students' abilities. Consumers love tests' apparent precision of measurement. And it is much easier to make a decision relying heavily on numbers than to make one relying heavily on seemingly subjective data, such as teachers' letters of recommendation or lists of extracurricular activities—even if the scores on these tests are nowhere near as valid as they appear to be. Skilled admissions officers, therefore, take into account the subjective as well as the objective factors, recognizing the need for a holistic evaluation of each applicant. They resist the temptation to do their job the easy way—by the numbers.

Anyone is susceptible to overinterpreting numbers. Some years ago I was giving a talk to an audience of people who drilled for oil. They were interested in finding people who would be skilled at predicting where oil could be found. As I was talking about our work, someone in the audience raised his hand and made a curious point. He said that their company had the same problem with clients that we had with admissions. Clients would often prefer that they drill for oil in places where there were quantitative indices indicating the likelihood of oil, even if those quantitative indices were known to be largely invalid. They would prefer to go with quantitative rather than superior qualitative information based on the judgments of experts, simply because it was associated with numbers. And they got a lot of dry holes.

Successful Test Takers Seem More Attractive as Applicants

People are attracted to others who are like themselves. We tend especially to like others who are similar to us in interpersonal attractiveness, who share our interests, who are in our ethnic group, and so forth. The tests that have been so highly valued since the 1960s have yielded a new generation of power-holders who look for others like themselves—that is, others who have high test scores.

During the era in which most people going to elite colleges were from socially elite families, admissions officers were themselves mostly from elite families. So they looked for people with similar backgrounds. Today, to be admitted to elite colleges, it helps to have high scores from either the SAT or ACT. As a result, some admissions officers had relatively high board scores, or work for faculty who did. So some of these admissions officers may look for applicants who, like themselves and their mentors, will continue the legacy they have created. Such methods of producing social stratification are hard to change. But they explain why increasing the diversity of admissions staff can increase the diversity of the matriculated student body.[7]

Which system for selecting college students is better—test scores or social class and wealth? It depends on whom you ask. People in positions of power tend to value whatever attributes got them into those positions. If you ask a Harvard professor who is making $150,000 a year and who has published 150 articles in her career, the professor might wax enthusiastically about the advantages of the standardized tests that helped her get to where she is. If you instead ask an entrepreneur who dropped out of school and is making $150 million a year, that individual might laugh in your face. She might well think that money is a better basis for making decisions than test scores.

Someone else might question both test scores and wealth as bases for decision making. Mother Teresa and Mahatma Gandhi led lives of relative poverty but made an enormous positive difference to the world. They or those who admire them might argue that much more important than test scores or family wealth is the set of positive ethical principles one brings to one's life, and one's willingness to act on them.

In fact, there is no one perfect set of criteria for admissions—family wealth or status, test scores, ethics, all might form bases for people's theories of what one should look for in a qualified college applicant. It is important, however, to consider some historical background on the issue. And in the past, one of the most important criteria was gender.

When I started at Yale, it was an all-men's school. The first year that women were admitted, there was widespread outrage among alumni. Yet within a short time, women were, on average, outperforming men in their academic work. And when I became president of the American Psychological Association, I would go to meetings of the board of directors and look at the pictures of all past presidents of the association. It was pretty obvious that they were overwhelmingly men. Some might take this to indicate that men were more fit than women for such an esteemed position. But given that graduate schools for most of the history of the country did not admit women, what is truly surprising is that any women made it to such a position.

Other groups have experienced discrimination in the United States. To take just one example, if you were born in 1800 as a slave, and had an IQ of 160, it bought you little: you still died a slave. By contrast, if you were born the first son of a plantation owner, and had an IQ of 80, it mattered little: you still inherited the plantation. The law of "primogeniture" guaranteed that the inheritance passed to the eldest son. And no doubt the eldest sons felt that the law was remarkably fair in its recognition of their special role in their family and society.

Research by Claude Steele shows that socially defined race still matters in our assessments of ability, independent of the actual tests. Steele and his colleague Joshua Aronson have done a series of studies in which both white students and black students were asked to take a difficult test of verbal ability. When the participants were reminded, even subtly, of their socially defined race as part of the test-taking process, there was a greater difference in performance between whites and blacks than when they were not so reminded.[8]

It may be hard for some of us to believe that variables such as test scores, parental wealth, sex, socially defined race, and caste still affect one's possibilities in life. But imagine for a moment that the biggest determinant of an applicant's place in society in general, and in the college sweepstakes in particular, was, say, height. What then?

This thought experiment is less absurd than it might seem. First of all, our society does use height to determine social outcomes. Taller people are, on average, more successful than shorter ones, particularly among males. CEOs, army generals, and other successful people are more likely to be taller than average height, perhaps because people seem to respond better to authority in tall people. Second, height actually has an advantage over test scores: everyone knows exactly what it is. For example,

I am about five feet, eleven inches tall. You know what that means, right? But do you really know what an IQ of 125 means, or an SAT score of 580? And are they really different, or do IQs and SATs largely measure the same thing? (Research suggests that they are indeed closely related measurements.)[9]

Some years ago, my colleague Douglas Detterman and I edited a book in which two dozen experts in the field of intelligence were asked to define intelligence.[10] How many different answers did we get? You guessed it: two dozen. Even experts cannot agree on what intelligence is. But there is virtually no disagreement regarding the nature of height.

Second, height is the same regardless of the instrument with which it is measured. You could measure me with any of several tape measures, yardsticks, rulers, or whatever, and within a tiny margin of error, I would be five feet, eleven inches. If you measured me with a metric tape measure, it would come out at about 1.80 meters, but that still converts perfectly to five feet, eleven inches, with no loss of information. Ability tests have more complicated outcomes. You can give me half a dozen different ability tests, and I most likely will end up with half a dozen different ability scores, some of which may not be very close to each other at all.

Third, height has a reassuring consistency over time that is lacking in ability-test scores. I am the same height today as I will be until I shrink in my golden years. In contrast, one can take an ability test one day, and the same ability test a day, a week, or a month later, and there is much less guarantee of consistency. On tests like the SAT, variations of more than a hundred points between one testing to another are, while not common, far from rare, and fifty-point variations are quite common.

Fourth, some students cheat on standardized tests. They write their answers on their hands or inside their shirtsleeves, store them in the bathroom and then seek permission to go there, bring in hidden PDAs, or whatever. With height, all of these temptations to cheat are reduced. Sure, students can cheat by wearing platform or elevator shoes, but such devices are easy to detect.

Fifth, you can't buy height. Conventional test scores are susceptible to modification if parents can afford to buy their students books, courses, or just a sound education. With height, you've got what you've got unless you have the misfortune to have been severely and chronically malnourished. In that case, college probably won't be in the cards anyway, at least in the United States.

So there you have any number of reasons why it makes sense to use height for admissions to college. Suppose that we do in fact adopt the simple, easy-to-use height test. Now, to get into Harvard, you might have to be about six feet, eleven inches. To get into Yale, perhaps you would need to be only six feet, ten inches, and one goes down all the way to Squeedunk, for which admission requires one only to be three feet, one inch, and Podunk, which requires a height of a mere three feet even. What would the result be?

Almost without doubt, twenty-five years later most of the CEOs, army generals, and other people of high position would be tall, and most of the flunkeys of the society would be short. And what would this prove? That society favors tall people, in much the same way that it favors rich people over poor ones, men over women, whites over blacks (or, in some societies, blacks over whites), people of one religion over people of another, higher castes over lower castes, and so forth. That is to say, it would prove nothing at all other than that people can devise their own methods of social stratification, as well as the means to enforce the self-fulfilling prophecies that they have created.

Ignoring Test Scores at One's Peril

In some schools, admissions officers are reluctant to admit students who do not have high test scores. If the students are unsuccessful, the admissions officers are afraid that they, and not the students, will be blamed.

Indeed, every year some students in any given freshman class are identified as being at risk for flunking out, and at some schools, deans may look back to their admissions records for clues as to what went wrong. Why are these students failing, whereas others are not? Suppose those examining the admissions records discovered that the students who were flunking out were all admitted because one particular admissions officer had given them high ratings, whereas no one else had. That admissions officer would justifiably fear for his or her job. So people in positions of authority, whether in a college, graduate school, law firm, or anyplace else, worry about the decisions they make, because these decisions matter. What can they do to protect their reputations in case the people they recommend end up failing?

One thing they can do is use decision-making criteria that will help insulate them from criticism. Test scores are such criteria. If students flunk out or fail to adjust, the admissions officers or other decision-making personnel can blame the tests for leading them astray. But if they ignore the test scores, they may feel that others will place the blame squarely on their shoulders. And because test scores do correlate positively with academic success, those who make admissions or hiring decisions actually are taking a risk when they admit or hire people with lower test scores. Afraid of their own perceived future culpability, they may decide that the potential costs of taking such a risk are greater than the potential benefits.

Pressure from Published Ratings

It would be hard to overestimate the effects that published ratings have on the behavior not only of colleges, but also of elementary and secondary schools. Many, and probably most, elementary and secondary schools are shamelessly teaching to the standardized tests their students will have to take. They have to—the No Child Left Behind Act has given them little choice. The federal and state governments have placed a lot of pressure on schools to show that students have mastered a wealth of academic knowledge that will not necessarily matter greatly in their later lives. Principals risk losing their jobs and school boards may well lose control over their schools if their students underperform.

In addition, because the results of various districts on these tests are publicized, they become excellent predictors of real-estate values, which are driven up in districts where test scores are higher. I know this from firsthand experience. Recently, my wife and I were looking for a house in the Boston area. Test scores in a given community were a terrific proxy for real-estate prices. If you knew the test scores, you pretty much knew the house prices, and vice versa.

While tests potentially divert schools from their responsibility of fully educating students, *U.S. News and World Report* and other magazines that publish ratings of colleges and graduate schools encourage the schools to set goals that raise ratings rather than educate students. Test scores matter a lot for these ratings, and moreover, they are more manageable than other criteria that are used to evaluate the schools, such as alleged national reputation, whatever that is. So schools work hard to increase their mean test scores, thereby giving more authority and power to the publishers of the tests. It is a very good time to be a test publisher, because if you can get your product entrenched in the marketplace, it is likely to produce a lot of money, regardless of what it happens to measure.

One could argue that tests are a means toward accountability, and that all the magazines and newspapers are doing is making these indices of accountability public. This argument is a good one, assuming that the measures of accountability are also good ones. And presumably, the measures are not terrible. They do not require, for example, knowledge of techniques of black magic or voodoo. But, as I will argue later in the book, the tests we use tend to be incomplete, and they often measure types of knowledge that will not necessarily be of great use in the workplace, or even in life more generally.

Colleges are eager to improve their *U.S. News and World Report* ratings as well as ratings by other media. Higher test scores improve ratings, whereas lower test scores risk lowering ratings, and, possibly, risk the jobs of those responsible for the lower ratings.

Superstitions and Self-Fulfilling Prophecies

Every once in a while, I am invited to give a talk in a highly desirable location, perhaps Arizona or New Mexico. The problem is that, after I give my talk, they send me home and rarely invite me again. I keep thinking it would be nice to get another invitation so I could spend more time in one of the more desirable vacation spots.

Suppose I open up a service that guarantees rain. Given the increasing scarcity of water resources, such a service is likely to have a bright future. I promise municipalities, states, really, anyone who will invite me, that if they contract with me to make it rain, I will make it rain or I will give them double their money back. So I finally wangle out that return invitation to visit Arizona.

When I get to Arizona, instead of giving a talk on college admissions or leadership or something about which I really have some knowledge, I do a rain dance. The question is whether, later in the day, it will rain. Given that I am in Arizona, that is scarcely likely. So the town that has invited me asks for double its money back. I explain that there has been a grave misunderstanding: this is Arizona; they can scarcely expect the rain dance to work in just one day. In an arid environment like this one, it may take weeks or even months for the rain finally to come. So every day I do the rain dance in the morning, and sightsee during the rest of the day. Eventually, it rains. I congratulate the people of the town on their good judgment in inviting me to make it rain, and I pack my bags and leave.

This little story may sound silly, but it is exactly how superstitions work. If you do a rain dance long enough, eventually it will rain. And if it never does, you won't be alive to tell the story much longer. You may reply that you don't believe in rain dances. I don't either. But the chances are you have some superstition that is equally powerful. For example, approach the first-floor elevator in an apartment complex or a busy office building and wait by the elevator. Sooner or later, someone in a hurry will come and push the elevator button, even though it is already lit, indicating that someone has already summoned the elevator. Why would anyone push the button when it already has been pushed? One reason is that elevators provide what psychologists call a 100 percent reinforcement schedule. If you press the button, the elevator always comes. So even though pressing an already lit button has no discernible effect, people keep pressing because they are always rewarded for doing so.

I may sound as though I am making fun of the superstitions of others, but I have my own. I wear a medal around my neck that my parents gave me forty-seven years ago. They told me it would bring me good luck. Does it? I have no idea. But I keep wearing it because I feel that, in general, I have had a good life, and the cost of wearing it is very small. Probably taking it off would have no effect, but what if it did? And that is precisely how superstitions maintain themselves, including in the academic realm.

Once society comes to believe that high test scores are a necessary condition for student success, its members continue to hold this belief even in the absence of evidence. When I was at Yale, some of my colleagues used to tell me that students with scores below 650 would not succeed in our graduate program. They pointed out that, in fact, all successful students had scores above that level. They were right: at the time, we refused to admit students with lower scores, so we never found out how they might perform. In colleges and universities, we have our own superstitions, and over time, we come to believe them, often thinking they are rational rather than fanciful.

Some superstitions are benign. For example, no one is hurt by my wearing a medal around my neck. But other superstitions have serious consequences. As a result of our overuse of testing, many students never get a chance to show what they could do if only they were given the opportunity. So students who do not fit the particular mold that the tests create suffer as a result of our certainty that the test results mean much more than they do.

I have experienced the effects of such superstitions personally. When I was young, I did poorly on IQ tests. I would like to believe that this was because of test anxiety, but who can say for sure? In the 1950s, when I was growing up, the elementary school I attended gave group IQ tests every couple of years. As a result of my low scores, my teachers thought I was stupid and I did too. They never came out and told us our IQ scores, but one could tell from the way teachers acted. In first grade, I was a mediocre student, which made my teachers happy because they got what they expected. I in turn was happy that they were happy, and in the end, everyone was quite happy. By second grade, I was slightly worse as a student, and in third grade, still worse. This is a fairly typical pattern. It is sometimes referred to as "cumulative deficit." Once low expectations set in, every year one performs a bit worse than the year before. Eventually, one is labeled a perennial loser.

Was I really a perennial loser? To the extent that there was a superstition that the low IQ scores ensured my poor academic performance, the superstition created a self-fulfilling prophecy, of which I was the victim. So academic superstitions are not victimless. They affect those about whom the superstitions are held. They also affect schools and society, because they cause students to underperform, and for talents to be lost to society.

I was lucky. In fourth grade, I had a teacher, Virginia Alexa, who saw beyond the tests in the same way that some college admissions officers do. She had high expectations for me, and she conveyed these high expectations to me. Just as I wanted to please my first-, second-, and third-grade teachers, I wanted to please her. In fact, I was extremely taken with her, and remember regretting only that she was so much older than I—and married.

So in fourth grade, I became an A student. My entire future trajectory changed as a result of just one teacher. But I have often asked myself: What would I have done if she had not been my teacher? Where would I be today? And when I was working in college admissions, I wondered how many of the students applying might have had far stronger records, if only they had had, as I did, a teacher who believed in them.

If this were just a story about me, one might write it off as a unique incident. But I see it all the time. Consider a story of a child whom I'll call Adam. When Adam was in elementary school, he changed from one school to another. Because the new teacher needed to place him in a reading group, school administrators gave him a reading test his first day in his new school, in much the same way that many colleges give language or math or other placement tests just as students arrive. At the risk of stressing the obvious, the first few days at a new school or on a new campus are not ideal days for giving tests. The students tend to be overwhelmed by the challenge of adapting to the unfamiliar environment, and their minds often are not on the tests they are given.

In Adam's case, he bombed the reading test, which meant that his school had a decision to make. It could follow the lead of his former school, which was essentially identical in quality to his new school, and put him in the top reading group. Or it could follow the superstition that a test tells all, and put him in the bottom group. The school put him in the bottom group, ignoring his former successful placement. He was being set up to fail.

After a few weeks, his teacher noticed that Adam was reading at a higher level than his classmates, and recommended that he be placed in a more advanced reading group. But the school, locked into the superstition that tests tell all, decided to ignore the recommendation and instead retest him. His reading test score was now at the level of the middle group, so the school put him in that group. Soon the teacher noticed that Adam was performing better than students in the middle reading group, so the school once again gave him the reading test. This time he scored at the level of the top group. Given the school's ardent belief in the superstition that the test tells all, one would expect the school then to place Adam in the top reading group. The school didn't. It left him in the middle reading group.

Adam's mother and father made an appointment with very high-level personnel in the school to discuss why he was being retained in the middle reading group. The teacher was there, as was the principal, the reading specialist, and a school psychologist. The school officials explained to the parents that although Adam had scored at the level of the top group, he was now a full book behind the students in that top group. If they were to move him to the top group, he would lack the skills that the other students had. The parents were incredulous. They reminded the school officials that he was behind because the school had initially placed him in the bottom group.

The parents offered to help Adam with his reading. If he brought the book home, they would work with him to help him catch up in his reading skills. The parents felt qualified to assist him; both were PhDs and worked in education. But the school explained that its policy was not to allow reading books to go home, and that therefore they could not help. The school staff members were determined to ensure that the self-fulfilling prophecy they created would come true.

One would like to believe that colleges and universities are above such superstitions, but they are not. Rather, superstitions are firmly entrenched in our entire educational system, from elementary school onward. Colleges and universities sometimes use SATs and related tests in much the same way that elementary and secondary schools use standardized achievement tests. Sometimes the logic used is laughable—or would be, if real students' futures weren't at stake.

At one point, when I was working for The Psychological Corporation, a testing company, a case was brought to our attention as a result of a complaint. A student was applying to a graduate program that, at the time, required a score of 25 on the Miller Analogies Test. This in itself was strange, because at the time the test had 100 items, each with four multiple-choice options, so 25 was the score one could expect to receive if one answered the questions at random. A student applied with a score that was below 25: she was unlucky in her responses. But the school admitted her anyway because she had other credentials that were excellent. She went through the program and was about to graduate with honors when she was handed an unwelcome surprise: she was told that, in order to graduate, she would have to retake the Miller Analogies Test and receive a score of at least 25 so she could meet the admissions requirement. Here the predictor—the test—was being given more weight than the criterion it was supposed to predict—university-level academic performance. Her complaint was that she should not have to retake the test. (The complaint later became moot when she took the test and received a score of 26. She graduated with her honors.) Such a practice may be atypical, but I have heard similar stories.

Academic superstitions do not have to be about test scores. In the case of a little girl whom I'll call Margaret, it can have to do with other measures that an authority figure decides are important. When Margaret finished kindergarten, her Montessori School teacher wanted to hold her back because the teacher was convinced that Margaret had not yet developed the social skills she would need to succeed in first grade. Margaret's parents persuaded the teacher otherwise and the teacher kindly promoted Margaret, who went on years later to study at an Ivy League college.

Some readers might wonder what all the fuss is about. After all, test scores do, on average, predict academic achievement, so why shouldn't schools use them for this purpose? I have no objection at all to tests used in this way. Indeed, testing can be useful in diagnosing students' strengths and weaknesses and in helping the students themselves to capitalize on their strengths and to improve in their areas of weakness.

The problem is that tests often are not used in this way. Some schools have cutoffs.[11] These cutoffs may be explicit, in which case they are publicized; or they may be implicit, whereby college officials know they exist but do not talk about them. For example, in some business schools, if one's GMAT score is below 600, one's chances of getting in are reduced to practically zero. Many undergraduate as well as graduate schools use formulas for determining admissions. The assumption is that such formulas will accurately predict, at some level, who will succeed and who will fail. And it is further assumed that using such formulas somehow makes the process "fair." Given the correlation of test scores with family income, it would be about as fair to plug family income into the equation instead of test scores.

Financial Considerations

This may sound ridiculous, but many schools—in fact, the large majority of schools—implicitly do include family income in the admissions equation. Those schools that are not "need-blind"— that is, which admit students in part based on financial-aid considerations—do take into account family income in making their decisions, whether formulaically or otherwise. For the most part, these schools would like to be need-blind: they just do not have the economic resources to reach their goal any other way.

Jesse Rothstein, an economist at Princeton University, has suggested that test scores essentially "launder" students' socioeconomic background.[12] Much of a student's SAT score is attributable to the quality of the high school that a student attends, which in turn is a function of socioeconomic class. So test scores essentially serve as an effective substitute, however subtly disguised, for one's family background on a student's record. For even though admissions officers try to take extenuating factors such as lower socioeconomic background into account when considering scores, neither they nor anyone else knows the full extent of this relationship.

The concept of socioeconomic status is not perfectly defined.

It refers to one's social standing in a way that takes into account social variables such as where one lives, economic variables like the wealth and income of the family, and educational variables such as educational background.

There are different views on why socioeconomic status correlates rather highly with test scores. The theories are not necessarily mutually exclusive. One theory is that children who grow up in higher socioeconomic circumstances are given more opportunities to learn the skills measured by the tests, and thus are in a better position to test well. A second theory is that the correlation is actually genetically determined.[13] The idea is that smarter people pass on genes to their children that make them smarter; these genes lead them to excel and to reach higher socioeconomic levels; and they then pass on these "success" genes to the next generation, continuing the cycle. Most likely, genetic and environmental factors interact, as is the case with many aspects of human behavior.

CLOSED SYSTEMS, CLOSED DOORS

Standardized "aptitude" tests can, to some extent, create a closed society.[14] They predict achievement because, to a large extent, they are achievement tests. The SAT Reasoning Test and the SAT subject tests (also called "SAT II's") are, in many cases, so similar that one cannot always distinguish them by their questions. Indeed, Binet's intelligence tests, created at the beginning of the twentieth century, were designed to predict school achievement, so they were created essentially as achievement tests for skills that students should have acquired by a particular age or grade. Thus tests create a closed system: ability test scores predict achievement test scores because they are achievement tests. And the allegedly high "validity" of the tests makes users happy, because they essentially predict scores on other tests like themselves but are labeled something else.

At different points in time, societies, including our own, have found different bases for social stratification. In earlier times in the United States, socioeconomic class was the primary criterion used to stratify students, for college admissions and earlier. Then test scores came to be used, and they seemed to be more "merit-based," except that they produced largely the same results as the socioeconomic class indicators—the results were just different enough to give the appearance that wholly different measures were being used. At various times, admissions officers have used gender, socially defined race, and caste as bases for admissions. They have then found, to their satisfaction, that the criteria they used predicted future outcomes. This was not a kind of thinking particular to admissions officers. They were reflecting the societal context in which they lived. Remember that not so long ago, very few whites would have even considered the possibility of an African American becoming president of the United States. In most countries around the world, electing such a leader still seems impossible.

Imagine that we, as a society, were still using medical tests that were largely the same as those used at the beginning of the twentieth century. Would you be concerned? If you have ever had anything beyond a common cold, you would have reason to be. We should be equally alarmed that, as a society, we are using tests of abilities and achievements that are roughly the same as those devised a hundred years ago.[15] Although our current ability and achievement tests are more refined, more sophisticated, and more carefully constructed, the deep structure of these tools remains unchanged. A narrow conception of intelligence seems to be prevalent in today's society because of what is referred to as a closed system. A closed system is self-contained, internally consistent, and difficult to escape. A closed system, once it is in place, becomes self-perpetuating and difficult to change.

The vicious circle created by such a system gave rise to *The Bell Curve* by Richard Herrnstein and Charles Murray, a book that looks at the history of intelligence and class structure in the United States.[16] According to Herrnstein and Murray's 1994 analysis, conventional tests of intelligence, on average, account for about 10 percent of the variation in various kinds of real-world outcomes. Although this percentage is not trivial, it is not particularly large either, and one then might wonder what all the fuss is about regarding the use of the tests. Of course, one might argue that Herrnstein and Murray have underestimated the percentage, but given their enthusiastic support for conventional tests, it seems unlikely they would underestimate their value. In fact, they may have overestimated the value of the tests for predictive purposes.

Clearly the tests have some value. But how much? In their book, Herrnstein and Murray refer to an "invisible hand of nature" that guides events so that people with high IQs tend to rise toward the top socioeconomic stratum of a society and people with low IQs tend to fall toward the bottom stratum. They present data to support their argument, and indeed it seems likely that, although many aspects of their data may be arguable, in U.S. society their argument holds true. For example, on average, lawyers and doctors probably have higher IQs than do street cleaners.

The problem is that although the data are probably correct, the theory behind the data is probably not. U.S. society is not as it is because of an invisible hand of nature, but rather because a closed system has been created. The United States and some other societies have created cultures in which test scores matter profoundly. High test scores are needed for placement in higher tracks in elementary and secondary schools. They are needed for admission to selective undergraduate programs. They are needed again for admission to selective graduate and professional programs. It is really quite difficult to imagine how a person could gain access to many of the highest-paying and most prestigious jobs if he or she did not test well.

This system is tragic in many ways. Students spend years in primary and secondary school working hard (or not so hard) to achieve their goals, and then do the same in college. Sometime during their career, they take a test that lasts three to four hours.

Then that test score ends up having a weight equal to those products of years of effort and dedication in the admissions decisions of college and graduate programs. If test scores were as valid as other achievements in predicting success, perhaps this system would make sense. But they are not.

Instead, the 10 percent figure of Herrnstein and Murray implies that IQ-like abilities matter some, but not much, for life success. Other abilities that are important for life may not be measured effectively by standardized tests. For example, the creative and practical skills that matter to success on the job typically are not measured on tests used to get into school. Society may be overvaluing a fairly narrow range of skills, even if that range of skills may not serve individuals particularly well on the job.

In a reductio ad absurdum of the whole IQ-testing mentality, the New London, Connecticut, police force rejected the applicant Robert Jordan for having too high an IQ.[17] His score, 125, though far from stellar, was well above average. The police force argued that someone with too high an IQ might get bored quickly and then decide to leave the police force, thereby wasting the city's money spent in training. Some might find it disconcerting that a police force would value mediocrity, but apparently, this one did. The potential policeman sued and lost.

It is scarcely surprising that ability tests predict school grades, because, again, the tests were originally designed explicitly for this purpose. This historical fact makes it obvious how the United States and some other societies have created closed systems. Certain abilities are valued in instruction, such as memory and analytical abilities. Ability tests are then created that measure these abilities and, thus, predict school performance. Then assessments of achievement are designed that also assess these abilities. Thus it's little wonder that ability tests are more predictive of school achievement than of success in the workplace. Within the closed system of the school, a narrow range of abilities leads to success on ability tests, in instruction, and on achievement tests. But these same abilities are less important later in life, for instance, on the job, when providing for a family, or when contributing to a wider community. The costs of this closed system are high. Closed systems seal off individual options and distort society, depriving many individuals of opportunities they should have. Society is also deprived of their talents. So why did such a closed system emerge?

In addition to the reasons for the development of closed systems mentioned earlier, there may be a unique historical explanation for why the tests we use are so narrow. An early intelligence theorist, Charles Spearman, active in the first decades of the twentieth century, believed that all there is to intelligence is what he called "general intelligence," or *g*. Belief in this general factor remains entrenched among many psychologists, even today.[18]

A BROADER UNDERSTANDING OF INTELLIGENCE

Many others, however, believe that there is more to intelligence than just one general ability.[19] For example, Howard Gardner has proposed eight "multiple intelligences"—linguistic (understanding what you read), logical-mathematical (balancing your checkbook), spatial (using a map to find your way around a new city), musical (keeping tune in singing a song), naturalist (observing and understanding patterns in the natural world), bodily-kinesthetic (kicking a goal in soccer), interpersonal (understanding other people), and intrapersonal (understanding yourself).[20] A theory such as Gardner's suggests that the tests we use for college admissions are too narrow, because they primarily assess only linguistic and logical-mathematical skills.

Furthermore, depending on the situation, attributes that have nothing to do with intelligence (at least, according to the present and most other definitions) can end up becoming conflated with intelligence, thereby skewing any test results. For example, I attended classes in a number of typical one-room elementary schools in Jamaica. There was no barrier separating the many classes in the single room, so the noise level was constantly high. I found myself wondering what Binet might have put on his intelligence test if he had wanted to calibrate it to measure future success for these students, and concluded that he might have decided to include a battery of hearing tests. One's ability to hear the instruction and the test questions, both of which were typically given verbally, was critical. In this situation, those who did not hear well, perhaps simply because they did not sit in the front center of the classroom, fared worse than those who could hear well.

The importance of hearing to measures of intelligence is not just hypothetical. When I mentioned my observation in a colloquium, an individual from Guyana commented that she had grown up in similar schools and had always wondered why the smartest students sat in the front of the class. In this case, sitting in front, where it was easiest to hear and to be engaged, may well have made students appear smart. The teacher probably did not think that good auditory (sensory hearing) abilities were a component of intelligence, but he or she might have easily conflated the effects of such abilities with intelligence. Similarly, students with poor vision who do not have the benefit of corrective lenses may appear to teachers and school staff to be not very bright.

The experience in Jamaica also points out one other important fact, namely, that much research on intelligence is based on the assumption that all students have an equal chance to succeed on ability tests and in school. In fact, they do not. For example, in a study done in Jamaica in 1997, my colleagues and I studied the effects of intestinal parasitic infections (most often, whipworm) on students' cognitive functioning.[21] Our study showed that infected students tended to do worse than other students on tests of higher-order cognitive abilities, even after controlling for possible confounding variables such as socioeconomic class. It also revealed that, although antiparasitic medication improved physical health, it had no effect on cognitive-ability test scores. Presumably, the deficits caused by the infection had built up over many years and were not alleviated by a quick-fix pill. Students who are parasitically infected find it hard to concentrate on their schoolwork because they do not feel well. The data showed that the cumulative effect of missing much of what happens in school probably cannot be reversed quickly. Indeed, students in all societies who suffer from health problems, including poor nutrition, or who feel unsafe at home or school, do not have equal chances to succeed.

Societies can and do use a variety of criteria to sort people. Some societies use caste systems—whether explicitly, as in India, or implicitly, as in the United States. Others use or have used race, religion, or parental wealth as a basis for sorting. Many societies combine criteria. After a system is in place, those who gain access to the power structure, whether through elite education or another means, are likely to look for others similar to themselves to place in positions of power—simply because there probably is no more compelling basis of interpersonal attraction than similarity. The result is a potentially endlessly looping closed system.

Why have we reached this point? First, the cart somehow came to be placed before the horse: commercial interests came into play before the science of assessment had much opportunity to develop. Second, a small number of commercial enterprises largely monopolize the testing business, and many of the researchers in the field (including myself) have either worked for, or have been supported financially or otherwise by, these organizations. Such organizations, like any others, will continue doing what is profitable for them. Third, we have been and continue to be entranced by the notion of accountability, while largely ignoring just how narrow our cognitive and educational measures of accountability are. Fourth, the tests have seemed roughly consistent with the notion of a general ability that pervades many psychological performances. And finally, by some measures, the tests have worked: they predict various kinds of success at some modest to moderate level. The question, then, is not whether these tests work at all, but rather, how we can improve the over-all process of student assessment.

It is tempting to blame the "evil" testing companies for the problems we have in admissions testing. But they are no better or worse than the large majority of other companies. They are there to make money. (Even the nonprofits are there to make money, although they have a different accounting system.) If custom-ers—the colleges and universities—were to insist on other types of tests, the companies would create them. But the colleges and universities are comfortable, for the most part, with what they have. Consequently, there is no one entity that is to blame for what we have today. Instead, we have a case of an inadequate system that has become entrenched because it benefits many powerful people and because, to date, the voices of those who do not benefit have not been forceful or persuasive enough to enact change.

CHAPTER 2

HOW WE GOT HERE:

THE TRADITIONAL

COLLEGE APPLICATION

What are the elements of a traditional college application? Which assessments are used, and how are they combined and weighted to arrive at an admissions decision? An essential tenet of educational and psychological testing is to use assessments in combination in order both to capitalize on their strengths, and, by averaging out possible errors, to compensate for their weaknesses.

HIGH-SCHOOL GRADE-POINT AVERAGE

Grade-point average (GPA) still is the most important factor in admission to most colleges and universities. It has many strengths as an assessment.

First, the best predictor of future behavior is generally past behavior of the same kind. For example, if someone has tended to overeat during holidays in the past, they probably will in the future as well. If someone has been charitable in the past, he or she probably will be in the future, too. And if someone has earned good grades in the past, he or she probably will do so again in the future. Because academic work forms a cornerstone of college education, and because failing academic work can cause a student to drop out early, it makes sense that college admissions offices would rely on high-school GPA as a fundamental basis for making their decisions.

A second strength is that high-school GPA, although a single number, actually represents the level of mastery of a wide range of skills. It reflects a student's academic ability, of course, because getting good grades requires students to acquire a knowledge base and then to reason with it. It further reflects the student's practical abilities: can the student understand what is expected of him or her, devise strategies for studying for different types of tests (such as multiple choice and essay), figure out what the teacher is likely to test, and budget the available time in a way that allows him or her to excel in not just one subject, but several? Moreover, high-school GPA reflects, as much as or more than anything else, motivation—the student's willingness to work hard to achieve high marks in school.

Third, GPAs are readily available. Nearly all schools calculate a GPA for their students, so the admissions office need not require anything extra of the student in order to get the information, except perhaps the student's permission to have it released.

The GPA, however, also poses challenges. First, high schools differ in their quality and in the quality of the students that attend them. In some high schools, having a 3.8 average may mean that the student has completed a highly rigorous selection of courses and has done extremely well in them. In other high schools, courses may be much weaker and the grades in them mean much less. Even within high schools, courses differ widely in how academically rigorous they are.

Second, high schools differ in what their grades mean. Long ago, "C" meant "average." In theory, roughly 8 percent of grades were A's, 24 percent were B's, 36 percent were C's, 24 percent were D's, and 8 percent were F's. Schools may have differed in the exact percentages used, but the term "gentleman's C" referred to the grade received by a student who did not work particularly hard and who made no effort to achieve at a level above the average. Today, by contrast, a C is often considered a disgrace. In fact, I have had any number of students complain about grades of A−. They want to be the best and anything less just will not do.

Third, the desire for high grades is partly a result of high motivation, but it also has been fueled by grade inflation. An A just does not mean as much anymore. Neither does a 4.0 average. With corrections introduced by schools for course difficulty and other factors, a 4.0 average may place a student in the upper portion of a high-school class, but nowhere near the top. Efforts are made every now and then to hold grade inflation in check, but such efforts have not been particularly successful.

Fourth, high schools differ in what courses even count toward the GPA. In one school, a course such as woodworking may not count at all; in another school it may count but be weighted only lightly; in another school, it may count the same as any other course. The school may indicate its methodology, but admissions officers typically are not going to recompute the whole GPA to give more value to certain courses.

Fifth, grades represent in some degree the skill of knowing what teachers want and giving it to them. Of course, students will have to do the same in college, but will they use the same skill? In a rigorous high school, the expectations of the teachers may correspond to those of college instructors—for example, students may be asked to think independently, debate appropriately with others, and conduct in-depth outside research. But in a less rigorous school, an A may mean simply that the student was well behaved and did exactly what he or she was told.

Some schools are familiar to admissions officers. When I worked in admissions at Yale some time ago, I felt I could interpret quite well the grades and GPAs from schools with which I was familiar—usually those that consistently sent a number of students to Yale over the years. But I also realized that my knowledge could bias me toward candidates from those schools.

After I was admitted to Yale, I went to work in the college's Office of Institutional Research under a psychologist, now deceased, who computed predicted grade-point averages. He was someone who even then, in 1968, represented a past generation of psychologists. He predicted GPAs using a hand calculator (and when computers came into use, and he found himself without a job, to my astonishment he took to checking the computer's calculations by hand). I discovered that he used a correction factor that took into account the high school one attended. Yale had been using percentage grades and the psychologist in charge would convert a student's grades in high school to expected percentage grades at Yale. In my case, for example, because I had attended a public high school that was largely unknown to him, he had automatically subtracted nine points. That meant that the highest predicted GPA I could attain was a ninety-one.

The psychologist in charge was only trying to do his job, albeit in an outdated way. But the problem that he was addressing is still not totally solved. When an admissions officer sees a GPA from an unknown school in rural Appalachia, or an inner-city high school known more for its disciplinary problems than for the academic achievement of its students, the admissions officer may make the same calculation in his or her head, perhaps not even quite consciously, that the psychologist had made explicitly. Schools that seek diversity may end up admitting some students from the unknown high schools. But only a few.

The problem of underrepresented schools has another origin: for these students, college may not seem like a viable option, and a selective college may not be something they even consider. This gap is, in part, due to inadequate resources for college guidance at the high schools. In addition, guidance counselors in some remote schools may not even be aware that their students have a chance of attending colleges that, to the counselors, seem out of reach.

The irony is that going to a more selective school does not necessarily mean that one will have to struggle more to achieve good grades. At the university level, for example, Harvard, among the most selective colleges in the United States, has been as wracked by grade inflation as anyplace else, and perhaps much more so than many of the community colleges with which it would never view itself as competing. Grade inflation has affected many high schools and private preparatory schools as well, including some of the most selective ones. The general point is that grades are hard to interpret, for a wide variety of reasons. Fortunately, admissions officers look for more.

CLASS RANK

Most high schools provide a measure of a student's rank in class—that is, how far he or she is from the top of the class. The information in class rank is partially but not wholly duplicative of the information in GPA. This is because class rank controls for the severity of the grading in the school. In one school, a B (3.0) average may place a student in the upper third of the class, whereas in another school, it may place a student well into the bottom half. The class rank partially adjusts for these differences in grading.

The class rank is always interpreted in the context of how many students are in the class, and is usually interpreted in the context of the school one attends. A class rank of one means a different thing at a highly competitive school than at a small rural school with students who are much less well-equipped academically. But school quality is not always factored in: for example, being in the top 10 percent of your high-school class in Texas guarantees admission to the University of Texas, regardless of the school you attend.[1]

Some high schools and private preparatory schools prefer not to rank their students. In fact, if there is a trend in recent times, it is toward high schools' not computing class rank. The advantage of such a decision is that it takes some pressure off students during their high-school careers. The disadvantage is that college admissions officers find it harder to evaluate applicants from such schools, so students could potentially be put at a disadvantage. If the school is known to the admissions officers, however, they may calculate, even implicitly, a rough class rank based on what they know about the school.

COURSE LOAD AND PROFILE

College admissions officers consider not just the numerical value of the GPA, but also the courses that make up that GPA. The course load and profile can tell the admissions officer quite a bit about the student's academic skills and motivation. Is the student taking very challenging courses or relatively easy ones? If a foreign language is expected by the college, how many foreign-language courses has the student taken, and how many languages has she or he studied? Has the student taken the requisite mathematics courses needed for college success? Are there special courses on the transcript, such as honors or Advanced Placement (AP) courses, if they are available in the student's secondary school? Is the student in a special program known for its rigor, such as the International Baccalaureate (IB) program? What kinds of electives has the student chosen? Information about the course load and profile can reveal information not available in the composite GPA.

At the same time, the admissions officer needs to factor in extenuating circumstances. Not all schools offer AP courses or the IB program; and even if they do offer AP courses, their offerings may be limited. Schools may also have various restrictions on who can take such courses. For example, in one school, AP courses may be available to virtually anyone, whereas in another school the courses may be available only to the very best students. So the admissions officer needs to factor in not just which courses were taken, but which were available to be taken. The admissions officer also needs to see the course profile in the context of the students' other activities. For example, students who are very involved in high-school sports may choose courses that will allow them to succeed academically even though they have to spend a lot of time on the playing field. The officer may or may not choose to view such extracurricular activities as compensatory for taking a lighter course load.

STANDARDIZED TEST SCORES

Much of this book is about standardized tests, so I will not repeat here what is covered elsewhere. In summary, there are two standardized tests that have a monopoly in the college-admissions market in the United States—the SAT and the ACT.

Consider some of the history. The College Board was created in 1901, and the first of its tests was given in that year. At that point, the tests involved essays measuring achievement in school subjects such as history, Latin, and physics. But the enterprise as we know it today did not get under way until June 23, 1926, when the first Scholastic Aptitude Test (SAT) was administered. The test was created by a Princeton psychologist, Carl Brigham, and it had sections related to antonyms, arithmetic, analogies, and paragraph reading, among other things. Administered to roughly eight thousand students, the test lasted only an hour and a half, despite having more than three hundred questions.[2] Significantly, the kinds of questions used then did not differ much from those used today, and the underlying skills that the tests measure have scarcely changed.

The name "Scholastic Aptitude Test" was later dropped in favor of "Scholastic Assessment Test," and this name in turn was later dropped in favor of simply using the acronym "SAT" without its meaning anything in particular. Different reasons might be given for this shift, but the most obvious one is that neither the College Board nor anyone else is quite sure what the test measures, because it is not based on any particular scientific theory of a psychological construct but rather on a pragmatic assessment of what will predict scholastic success in college.

The SAT Reasoning Test has three parts, now called critical reading (formerly the "verbal" section), mathematics, and writing.[3] The critical reading section contains two types of items, sentence completion and passage-based reading. Sentence completion measures the student's word knowledge and understanding of how words fit together to form a comprehensible sentence. An example might be "The Parliament _____ the bill and, as a result, it _____ the law, resulting in a steep increase in the taxes citizens paid to the Crown." Options might be (a) rejected . . . enacted, (b) passed . . . became, (c) discussed . . . accepted, (d) disputed . . . nullified. Passage-based reading, by contrast, measures one's ability to read a long passage and understand and analyze it. And the critical reading section assesses the student's understanding of vocabulary in context, literal comprehension, and ability to engage in extended reasoning that goes beyond simply remembering what one has read. In some sections, test takers may be asked to compare two passages. Content generally covers the natural sciences, social sciences, humanities, the arts, and personal narratives. The SAT critical reading test is scored on a scale from 200 to 800.

The SAT writing test has two sections, one of which measures grammar, English usage, and choice of words in contexts, and the other of which is an essay that requires the student to take a point of view and defend it.[4] The multiple-choice section is scored on a scale from 200 to 800, and might show a sentence or paragraph and ask how it could be improved, or ask whether there is a grammatical error in a sentence. The essay is scored in a largely formulaic way. It is not designed to measure creativity in writing but rather the mechanical skills of knowing how to set up an argument, carry it through, and draw it to a conclusion. Thus, for better or worse, it is highly trainable. In a sample essay on the College Board website, students are asked whether memories help or hinder one's ability to learn from the past and succeed in the present. Students have just twenty-five minutes to write their essays.[5]

According to the College Board website, an ideal essay develops a point of view on the issue at hand, in this case, the role of memories in learning from the past.[6] It shows excellent critical thinking, and uses evidence and examples that help to bolster the argument being made. The essay must be exceptionally well organized, focused, and systematic in its development of an argument, and needs to include a variety of sentence structures. Finally, it should show nearly flawless use of words, grammar, and syntax. It is scored on a scale from one to six by each of two readers.

The SAT mathematics section has three parts that assess the student's knowledge of numerical operations, algebra, geometry, probability and statistics, and data analysis (for example, understanding and interpreting a graph). The highest level of difficulty tests material that would be covered in the third year of college-preparatory mathematics. The test has both multiple-choice and free-response items. Students are encouraged to use a calculator, and the test is not intended to measure recall of basic formulas; indeed, these basic formulas are provided. The test is scored on a scale from 200 to 800.

The second of the major college admissions tests, which tends to be used more in the Midwest and the South of the United States, is the ACT, which traditionally stood for American College Test but, like the SAT, now goes just by its acronym.[7] The ACT was created as a competitor to the SAT by Everett Lindquist, and was first used in the fall of 1959. It supposedly measures achievement more directly than does the SAT, but in fact the SAT subject matter tests are even more direct measures of achievement than is the ACT. The ACT, traditionally, has consisted of four subtests: English, mathematics, reading, and science reasoning. It also now includes an optional writing test. Scores range from 1 to 36 on each of the subtests as well as for the overall composite score, which is an average of the other tests. If the test taker takes the writing test, it is not included in the composite.

The English test requires forty-five minutes and covers English usage, similar to the multiple-choice part of the SAT writing test. The mathematics test lasts sixty minutes and includes algebra, plane geometry, coordinate geometry, and trigonometry questions. Calculators can be used. The reading test lasts thirty-five minutes and measures reading comprehension for four passages, including fiction, social science, humanities, and natural sciences. The science reasoning test lasts thirty-five minutes and requires the test taker to understand scientific writing and representation of scientific data. The writing section is thirty minutes long and involves a social issue that is relevant to high-school students.

It is easy to see why the SAT and the ACT are popular among college admissions officers and other administrators and faculty. The tests have several positive features. First, the tests measure skills that are relevant to college success. Students will need to read a tremendous amount of material in college, and they will need to understand and analyze it. Moreover, the material they will read will be in a variety of fields like those sampled on both the SAT and the ACT. College students will also have to know high-school mathematics in order to succeed in college math and science courses. They will need to be able to write well in order to complete essays on examinations as well as term papers and the like.

Second, the tests seem to provide a common metric across different students and schools. An SAT score of, say, 600 refers to the same number of correctly answered questions (after correcting for guessing) in one school as in another. In contrast, the GPA may mean very different things in different places.

I say "seem" to provide a common metric because a given score does not really mean exactly the same thing for each student who achieves it. One student may have grown up as a native English speaker with a lot of books in the home and highly educated parents who were able to educate the child in a way that would help maximize scores on the tests. Another student may have grown up with a foreign language as a native language, or even with parents who do not speak English at all. Another student may have had few books in the home and parents who were not able to provide an enriched educational experience. Admissions officers are trained to take such differences into account, but no one can do so perfectly because no one knows exactly what the effects of different upbringings are. Moreover, the first student likely will be at an advantage in college by having mastered the skills to achieve high grades. So the admissions officer must decide just to what extent he or she wants to take the background differences into account.

Third, the college does not have to pay for the test—the student applicants do. And finally, the tests give the appearance of being objective, so that colleges do not have to worry that the results are a reflection of who happens to be scoring them. The possible exceptions to this are the results of the writing tests, but even those are scored in ways that deliberately overlook novel, imaginative responses in the search for elements that can be measured somewhat objectively.

With all these advantages, why would anyone in his or her right mind not weigh the SAT or the ACT heavily (although certainly not exclusively) in admissions decisions? Well, for one thing, although the tests measure skills relevant to college success, they do not measure all such skills. Students need practical, commonsense skills to know how to study and organize their time. They need metacognitive or self-understanding skills to recognize their own strengths and weaknesses and how they might improve. They need motivational skills and attitudes to get themselves to work hard. And they need creative skills to generate novel ideas.

In addition, exactly how common is the metric provided by standardized test scores? I mentioned earlier that scores can mean different things for different individuals. Can the meaning of a given score vary by group as well?

In our studies of various ethnic groups living in San Jose, California, Lynn Okagaki and I found that each group had a rather different idea of what it means to be intelligent. Teachers tended to reward those children who were socialized into a view of intelligence that happened to correspond to the teachers' own.[8]

In any culture, practical intellectual skills matter for predicting adaptation to everyday environments. But a child growing up in inner-city Detroit, generally a low-income part of Michigan, faces challenges different from those of a child growing up in Grosse Pointe Farms, a generally wealthy suburb of Detroit, and parents socialize their children to develop the skills they need to face the challenges of their own environments. So the SAT actually may measure somewhat different skills for different children, depending on which skills the parents emphasized as the children were growing up. For example, the SAT mathematical test measures different skills for someone who has learned algebra and geometry than for someone who has to figure out the answers without that knowledge.

It is also important to realize that although the college does not pay for standardized testing such as the SAT or the ACT, students do. If we add up the costs of multiple test-takings, of books that parents buy for their children to help them prepare for the tests, and of courses or tutors, the costs become nontrivial. Moreover, there is also the "opportunity cost" to students who attend high schools that integrate what amounts to SAT preparation into their curricula. That is, the time the students spend preparing for these tests is time they are not spending doing other things that might be more worthwhile, such as engaging in athletics, creating art projects, studying music, or even reading literature instead of memorizing vocabulary words.

The ACT and, more recently, the SAT, offer students score choice—that is, they can choose which scores to send to colleges. But score choice poses a bit of a dilemma. Is a student who receives a 550 and a 650 on, say, the math SAT, really better than a student who twice receives a 600? The student who received the disparate scores can report only the 650 and thus look somewhat more skilled mathematically than the student who received the 600 twice. But is the student really more skilled? The average scores of both students are the same. One interpretation, of course, is that the 550 merely represented a "bad day." But error of measurement goes both ways—it can result in scores that are too low or too high. So score choice may skew the information available to colleges. It also poses another dilemma. If the student need only report highest scores, it encourages students to keep retaking the test—and paying for it—in the hope that he or she will hit the jackpot, securing a score that is appreciably higher than the other ones he or she has received.

Do we overvalue objectivity in tests? Consider the oft-told story of a man who is frantically looking at night for his lost keys. A police officer sees him looking and offers to help. Fortunately, the area where the man is looking is the one place that is well illuminated. The police officer and the man look for quite a while, with no success. Finally the police officer asks, "Are you sure you lost the key here?" To which the man responds: "Why, no, I lost them over there. But it is pitch black there, so I'm looking here where the light is better."

In standardized testing, we have tended to measure what is easy to measure. Arguably, this seemed right and proper in the 1920s, because testing was just starting out and it was impressive, at that point, that the testers could measure anything in a standardized and useful way. But the years passed and little changed. In testing, we have looked where the light is best, but in doing so, we have ignored what may well be the most important keys.

The so-called objective tests do serve a purpose in college admissions. But there is no need to limit ourselves to such tests. The best assessments use a variety of different assessment methods. Ideally, college admissions officers would combine the traditional objective assessments with others that, although more subjective in their scoring, allow students better to show the range of skills they possess.

Testing companies like the Educational Testing Service (ETS) and ACT are moving ahead with several projects to measure some of these other skills, such as the ETS Personal Potential Index, which seeks to measure skills beyond what the Graduate Record Examination (GRE) measures. One would hope that more and more assessments would move in this direction, and that they would become a more important part of admissions processes, for undergraduate as well as graduate admissions.

THE COMMON APPLICATION

Before the mid-1990s, each college had its own separate application, and students had to do a lot of repetitive work, filling out the same information again and again on multiple applications. Today, the Common Application is used by many colleges to save applicants this trouble.[9]

The Common Application asks for personal and family demographic information; test scores; lists of athletic or other honors and academic distinctions; principal extracurricular, volunteer, and family activities; paid work experience, if any; and future plans.[10] It also gives the applicant an opportunity, in 150 words, to elaborate on one of his or her activities. A longer, 250-word essay can be either open-ended, with the applicant choosing what he or she wishes to write about, or based on a prompt, such as to write about an experience one has had or a viewpoint to which one subscribes. Because the Common Application serves such diverse and heterogeneous applicants and colleges, the essay questions are pretty much "one size fits all." The application also asks about disciplinary history and any additional information the applicant may wish to provide.

Forms are included with the application that are designed to be given to one's teachers and to the guidance counselor (or equivalent). The teacher form asks about attributes such as academic achievement, intellectual promise, maturity, motivation, leadership, and integrity. It also asks for an overall rating. The guidance-counselor form includes a question about how class rank is computed, as well as a request for academic, personal, and overall evaluations of the applicant.

The Common Application does a good job of organizing a wide variety of information about the applicant in a way that can be used by many different colleges and universities. Moreover, it cuts down enormously on the work that applicants need to do in order to apply to multiple schools.

Yet there are some problems with the Common Application, as there probably would be for any application of its kind. First, as mentioned earlier, the essays have long been fairly standard and open-ended. Consequently, there has been an opportunity for unscrupulous merchants to build up banks of successful essays and sell them to students applying to colleges. There is little one cannot buy on the Internet these days. At best, students may use such essays as models. At worst, they may recycle old essays and use them as their own. The extent to which this dishonest practice occurs is unknown.

A second feature of the Common Application is that the essay topics do not particularly encourage creative responses (nor are they even designed to do so). Rather, they encourage students to spend years "building up records" that then can translate into college admissions success. As a result, the experience in high school and even earlier can become largely about building a record for college. In some cities, such as New York, the competition starts early, with children vying for places in kindergartens whose graduates tend to win placement in the city's more prestigious private schools. At least in some circles, the college admissions game begins before students even enter elementary school.

A third feature of the Common Application is that recommendations, like grades, have become inflated over the years. Topnotch ratings of students by teachers and guidance counselors have become more common, making it harder for the colleges to distinguish among applicants. This difficulty is not limited to the Common Application, but neither does this application provide a remedy to this vexing problem.

A fourth feature is that although teachers are asked to give a number of distinct ratings for the student, the ratings in fact suffer from what is often known as a "halo effect." This simply means that, if the teacher has a generally positive impression, most of the ratings turn out to be quite positive, and if the teacher has a generally negative impression, most of the ratings turn out to be less favorable, at least for a very selective college. Thus although it would be nice to receive distinct ratings for each of the rated elements, one rarely does. Rather, they reflect a general glow that the applicant emits in varying degrees. In the end, the written comments are often more helpful than the summary ratings.

A fifth feature is that the ratings can mean very different things in very different schools. The top student in Schnoginville may indeed be the best that the town has seen in the past ten years, but he or she may be competing with students who are not very competitive. The result, as discussed elsewhere, is that admissions officers may take more seriously recommendations from those schools and guidance counselors whom they know and trust.

INTERVIEWS

Interviewing practices differ widely from school to school. Some colleges do not offer interviews. Others do, but through alumni groups only. And still others offer on-campus interviews, but they may or may not use the interviews to evaluate candidates. Some years ago, when I worked in admissions at Yale, I did a cost-benefit analysis of the Yale Admissions Office interview.[11] Somewhat to my surprise, I found that the interview really did not count very much in the admissions decisions. The admissions officers realized that the interview is of limited value. It can help spot a few outstanding candidates, and some real duds. But as I discovered myself when I conducted college interviews, most of the applicants look good but not terribly well distinguished from the rest. Curiously, however, when applicants were asked to evaluate how well they had done, they thought they did much better than they did. And perhaps because they thought they presented themselves so well, they had a very positive impression, overall, of the interview experience. As a result, I recommended retaining the interview, primarily for public-relations purposes.

Alumni interviewers enable colleges to reach out to large numbers of applicants in ways that in-house interviews do not, but the range of talent among the interviewers is great, as is the range of standards to which they hold the applicants. It often is hard to know just what to make of the reports. Indeed, when I applied to Yale, my alumni interviewer was from another generation in which the values of the university had been very different. It was unlikely that he would have even known what the school was looking for in the modern age of 1967.

Interviews sometimes feel more valid than they are, because it is often difficult to separate self-presentational skills from the more basic attributes of the person.[12] Self-presentational skills do matter in life, so having the interview may predict the kind of impression a person will make on others, at least early on. They will be a disadvantage, however, for young people who may be slow to warm up or who feel intimidated by the interview setting. Like everything else, the interview has its strengths and its drawbacks as a means of assessing an applicant's characteristics.

EXTRACURRICULAR ACTIVITIES

Extracurricular activities form an important part of the application for many universities. They are considered important because they potentially reveal aspects of the applicant's personality and character that would otherwise not come to light. Admissions officers often are interested in seeking future leaders and productive citizens, and they know that test scores and grades only tell one so much. Extracurricular activities might speak directly to other qualities.

Not all schools count extracurricular activities. Some schools, especially state ones, are much more interested in class rank or a combination of class rank and test scores. In most of Europe, extracurricular activities do not count at all. Whether to count them depends as much on one's philosophy of admissions as anything else.

Even in the United States, colleges generally do not weigh extracurricular activities as much as they value test scores and grades. Why not, if such activities are among the few measures of character? Because self-reporting of extracurricular activities brings up several important questions, including:

- Are extracurricular activities relevant to whether a student will succeed academically? The first priority of the college or university is to ensure that the student can do the academic work at the institution. It is of no use to admit someone with a stellar extracurricular record who will flunk out after one semester. And in selective colleges, admissions officers seek students who will not merely pass their courses, but excel in them. Extracurricular activities generally do not say much about an applicant's ability to do the academic work of the school.
- Just how meaningful was the applicant's participation in the activity? It is hard to quantify extracurricular participation. Suppose, for example, the applicant reports having been president of the debating club. Questions then arise. Was he or she really president of the club? If so, how big a job was it? For example, how many members were there on the team, how much time did the student invest, and how many events were there? And what did the student actually do in the activity? Was he or she an active president who moved the club forward, or was the activity largely passive, serving to fill up a college application but little else? Ideally, the combination of sources of information will answer these questions, but not always. And although admissions officers can assign ratings to such activities, these ratings can seem subjective in comparison with test scores and grades.
- How many opportunities did the school provide? At some

schools, there may be room for everyone to be president of a club, whereas at others, there may be little opportunity for a student to shine in clubs or other after-school activities.

- Who wrote the description of activities? There is always the risk that the description of activities was written by someone other than the applicant, which would not only be inappropriate, but also would increase the chances that the description is inflated or flat-out wrong.

LETTERS OF RECOMMENDATION

Letters of recommendation provide an opportunity for teachers, guidance counselors, and occasionally others to provide information that may be obtained no other way. They can tell the college about a student's academic performance, abilities, initiative, curiosity, character, motivation, and the like—all from the viewpoint of someone who works directly with the student, often on a daily basis, and knows him or her well.

Sometimes, however, letters of recommendation are not nearly as useful as they could be. Why?

- Just as grades have been subject to inflation, so have letters of recommendation.
- Letter writers, even if assured the letters of recommendation are confidential, may worry that if they are less than positive they can be sued later. Their worry may or may not be justified. Although the confidentiality of letters is protected under the Buckley Amendment if the student signs an access waiver, there are no absolute guarantees. I was once burned myself when I wrote a supposedly confidential letter and then found out that the student about whom I had written had nevertheless learned the contents of my letter. Leaks do happen, even if only rarely.
- Some letter writers do not know the students as well as would be desired, especially if the writers are responsible

for very large numbers of students. Even if the letter writers know the students, they may not know about all of the attributes on which they are asked to comment.

- Although there are often multiple ratings that can be given to students, there can be a halo effect, which as explained earlier will cause all or almost all of the ratings to be similar. Halo effects are common not only in letters of recommendation, but also in many other kinds of ratings that people make.[13]

- Some letter writers are very experienced in writing letters of recommendation to competitive colleges and know better how to get the result they intend. They are experts at coded messages that downplay or obscure negative attributes while accentuating the positive. Other letter writers, say from high schools that send only a few students on to selective colleges, may not understand the system, so their letters may not give the student this added benefit. Admissions officers, too, are inclined to weigh more letters from schools and counselors they know and respect, which may give an edge to students who come from schools that have sent multiple students to that college.

The bottom line is that letters, like all other indicators, have strengths and weaknesses and have to be considered in the context of all available evidence.

TACIT FACTORS

There are other factors that affect admission that are not specifically part of the admissions application. They are factors that may weigh in a decision, even heavily, but that are tacit rather than explicit. These factors may include things such as the applicant's gender; ethnic affiliation; geographic origin; religion; specialized skills in areas like athletics, music, drama, or visual arts; and personal connections to the university, such as through parents or other relatives who work at the university or are alumni or large donors.

Many colleges and universities will declare that they seek diversity among their students but will not elaborate beyond that statement, and with good reason. If they become too specific, they risk legal entanglement. Diversity is genuinely a good thing: you can learn things from someone whose upbringing was very different from yours that you could never learn from someone who grew up next door. But seeking diversity is rarely straightforward.

At a university that is, say, a major Division I competitor in varsity athletics, anyone with half a brain knows that athletes receive different consideration than do non-athletes. Schools differ in just how much extra consideration they will give applicants who are athletes, but most do weigh athletic and other skills in their assessments.

Different people will give different justifications for these special categories. Usually they are grouped together under "diversity," although sometimes preferences impede diversity as, for example, in the case of facilitated acceptance for children of people who are well connected. As I write, there has just been a nationally covered scandal at a major state university regarding a special list that existed for children of well-connected parents. What amazed me was not the scandal but the number of people who acted as though they did not realize what was going on. The truth is, what happened at this state university happens every spring, in one form or another, at many other colleges and universities. Such patronage risks perverting the whole purpose of college and university admissions—which is supposedly to admit the best candidates. But it is very common.

In the case of special talents, one might argue that particular applicants should be accepted because of their unique ability to contribute to the university. For example, a given athlete might not be a top academic performer, but he or she is good at something that matters to the college or university. That something happens to be perceived as increasing alumni interest and participation in the school and probably financial donations as well. University athletics are a big business. Wins enhance donations, sometimes greatly, as well as ticket sales, which in turn enhance university revenues. Is it right to admit students because they enhance university revenues? It depends on whom you ask. Personally, I think such policies, at least when taken to extremes, lead universities down paths they will come to regret. In Europe, athletic prowess counts for nothing in college admissions. But in the United States, where there are teams and the college or university has a stake in their success, it would be difficult to remove athletic considerations from the admissions procedures in some universities. Moreover, athletics provides one way to build leadership skills among students.

Pragmatically, the temptation to succumb to various pressures is enormous—even though it can be, and is, overcome. At one of the universities where I have worked, a problem emerged when the child of a major potential donor was being considered for admission but was unqualified. The admissions office was aware of the enormous stakes involved. And it did try to find reasons to admit the child. In the end, however, he was rejected. The university was willing to consider bending its standards a bit, but it wasn't willing to break them. The donor was furious and said he would never donate again, and he hasn't. So the decision to reject was probably costly to the school. There was only one justification for the negative decision, really—it was the right thing to do.

Most such cases, though, are not black and white but instead gray. Perhaps the first oboist has just graduated and the orchestra desperately needs another. Or perhaps the quarterback on the football team has graduated and needs to be replaced. Perhaps students came from forty-nine states the previous year and accepting a certain candidate would mean that the university could claim that it had students from all fifty states. Or perhaps a valued faculty member who is supremely rational in his physics work threatens to find another job unless his daughter is admitted. In admissions, ideals are continually bumping into reality, and the chosen solution often is not perfectly principled but ultimately is made for pragmatic reasons. Admissions is probably not a good place for idealists who cannot compromise, nor for pragmatists who lack ideals.

CHAPTER 3

ALTERNATIVE ADMISSIONS

PRACTICES

A number of different proposals have been made to address the problems inherent in college admissions and to think of admissions in a fresh way. Some of these paradigms are still in the idea stage, whereas others are already in use, alone or in combination with others.

AFFIRMATIVE ACTION

Probably the most well-known proposal is affirmative action, which gives people from historically underrepresented groups opportunities to increase their representation in colleges or other institutions.[1] For example, if an institution has historically had a paucity of women or African Americans, affirmative action would provide a means for increasing the representation of members of these two groups within the institution. Affirmative action has been very successful in helping institutions reach their goal of increased representation among targeted groups, and many institutions today would be extraordinarily lacking in diversity were it not for affirmative action.

A disadvantage of affirmative action is that it is not fully based on the merits of the individual. That is, past discrimination against a student's group is considered part of the application process, but he or she may or may not be more qualified than someone else not admitted as a result of that past discrimination.

"Diversity" may sound like a politically correct buzzword, but to those of us who work in universities, it is much more than that. Much, or even most, of the learning at college goes on outside of the lecture hall, as students interact in academic discussion groups, as part of their extracurricular activities, or while just "hanging out." If students are all from similar backgrounds, their ability to learn from each other is greatly reduced, because they will tend to share assumptions and even entire ideologies. For example, consider the extreme case of a class composed entirely of students from New York and New Jersey. During the years I was at Yale, it was clear that we could build the entire entering class of qualified students from these two states. Would such a class have the diversity to ensure that students could learn from each other if they wished to?

When I started college, my roommate was from Atlanta, Georgia. Other students on my floor were from Pennsylvania, Texas, Illinois, Maine, New York, and Louisiana. Part of what made that freshman year a superb learning experience was that I became friends with students from places that to me were, before, mysteries. I had never met, much less become friends with, people from most of those states.

As usual, however, when it comes to affirmative action the devil is in the details. Exactly how does one go about increasing the representation of members of groups that traditionally have been underrepresented?

The first problem is figuring out what underrepresentation even means. Typically, it means that the proportion of individuals in the institution is lower than that in the population. But by this measure, most institutions have over- and underrepresentation of some groups. For example, most colleges have more students who hail from the same state or from nearby states than from faraway locations. But what are we to make of this fact, exactly? If, for example, students from New York City are overrepresented at New York University or Columbia University, it may be simply because more and/or better students apply from New

York than from other states or regions. How far does a college wish to go with apparently discriminatory standards in order to assuage problems of underrepresentation?

A second problem is ascertaining exactly what constitutes a "group." Are Hispanic Americans a group? The answer is complicated because Cubans, Puerto Ricans, and Mexicans, for example, have less in common culturally than a single label might imply. Similarly, Asian Americans from Vietnam and China or of Vietnamese or Chinese descent may have relatively less in common culturally than a single label would suggest, and Asians from Kazakhstan might have even less in common with the first two groups. Indeed, the common group label hides differences that may make two Asian Americans, for example, culturally more distant than two Anglo-Americans from different parts of the United States. So while it is admirable that admissions offices promote diversity by admitting members of diverse groups, they have to reflect carefully on just what they mean by a "group."

The problem is compounded in a society that has traditionally wanted to view itself as a melting pot. We do not have good definitions either of "groups" or of what it means for groups to be "underrepresented." And even if one is able to achieve greater representation of groups that are underrepresented, the melting-pot effect that diversity is intended to encourage—students of different backgrounds working together for a common good— may or may not happen. In many colleges and universities across the country, students of different backgrounds matriculate and then proceed to self-segregate. The result is a class or college that looks diverse on paper, but is not as diverse in terms of actual student interactions.

Under- and overrepresentation may also derive from various groups having, on average, different levels of education. Two groups in the United States with higher than average levels of educational attainment are Asians and Jews. Their high levels of educational attainment may lead to their "overrepresentation," relative to population figures, in colleges and universities. Seats taken up by members of these groups are, in a sense, taken away from seats that could have been occupied by members of underrepresented groups. But would a college want to vary its admissions standards to achieve particular numbers of members of particular groups? And can an institution do so legally? The issue of the academic credentials of candidates from underrepresented groups has been particularly thorny, and has given rise to a number of lawsuits.

These considerations do not, in themselves, argue against (or for) affirmative action. They merely point out that the issues are complex and that people of goodwill may have widely differing opinions. In implementing affirmative action, it helps to have a broad view of what constitutes potential for success. The system I shall propose later can be used with affirmative action to provide such a broad view.

Diversity is not always benign. When someone is admitted in order to increase the diversity of the incoming class, someone else is not admitted. So the risk is that in admitting the applicant from the fiftieth state so that the university can claim students from all fifty states, or the football player, or the oboist, someone else who was as qualified or more qualified in other ways will be excluded. Students of certain Asian ethnicities, for example, have tended in recent years to have especially high grades and test scores, but because they are not considered an "underrepresented" group, they may yield a place in admissions to someone who is so counted and who may have what appear to be weaker credentials. I do not claim to have a simple solution to this conundrum, and anyone who does is probably not trustworthy. Our admissions systems will always favor certain groups over others, depending on what criteria are in favor at a given time. The goal ought to be to make these systems as equitable as possible, realizing that complete equity is a pipedream. The proposal in this book for achieving equity addresses this issue by promoting admissions made on the basis of merit, but merit that is more broadly conceived than in the past.

FORMULAIC ADMISSIONS

The world of formulaic admissions is the polar opposite of the world of affirmative action. Institutions that use formulaic admissions usually combine standardized test scores with class rank or GPA in such a way that yields an overall merit score. Such a procedure is used at some state schools, including, until recently, the University of California, and currently, the University of Texas, which automatically admits students from Texas who are in the top 10 percent of their high-school class.

Although formulaic admissions sound rather cold, they do have clear advantages, namely predictability, uniformity, and objectivity. They clearly specify which students are admissible and which are not. They clearly specify the criteria for admissions, operationalize those criteria, and then apply them in a uniform and objective way to their applicants. One is spared the endless arguments over how to define groups, which groups to favor, and how one can justify rejecting students who may, in obvious ways, be highly qualified.

If formulaic admissions are so straightforward, why are they rarely used by private institutions? For one thing, they severely limit the criteria that serve as the basis of admissions. Few admissions officers would argue about the usefulness of high-school GPA, and most would accept that standardized test scores are also helpful. But admissions would be very narrowly conceived if only those two measures, or others like them, were used for making decisions. Many people who work in admissions believe that an applicant's ability to succeed, even academically, is very narrowly measured by standardized tests. These tests do not measure creativity, motivation, passion for learning, and other skills and attitudes that are important for academic success. Moreover, to the extent that the goal of admissions is to admit people who will be active citizens and leaders of society, high-school GPA and standardized test scores seem to miss the mark almost entirely.

In addition, formulaic admissions assume that a given score or GPA means the same thing for different people. But is a GPA of 3.8 or class rank of the top 10 percent the same in a high school that is barely competitive as in one that is highly competitive? Does an SAT score of 650 mean the same thing for a student who grows up speaking English as a native language in an upper-middle-class community, versus one for whom English is a second or even third language who grows up in a challenging inner-city situation?

Finally, what if formulaic admissions lead to a class that is extremely uniform in terms of background or ethnicity? It seems that formulaic admissions give an appearance of objectivity, but even as this strategy solves some problems, it creates others.

OPEN AND LOTTERY-BASED ADMISSIONS

Yet another option is open admissions. If there are more applicants than there are slots, then a lottery is used to determine who will get one of the available spaces. This system is widely used in continental Europe, and at this writing, Hugo Chávez, president of Venezuela, has decreed that his country should change from exam-based admissions to open admissions. Community colleges generally use open admissions or something close to it, and various commentators have proposed using lottery-based admissions for selective colleges.[2] Jerome Karabel, a distinguished scholar of higher education at the University of California, Berkeley, recently proposed a lottery for admission to prestigious colleges limited to those with strong academic credentials.[3] Of course, the question remains: what constitutes strong academic credentials? School grades are probably the most central measures of such credentials.

Those who support open admissions may argue that it is the

only democratic system for deciding who should get a seat in the university. To give everyone an equal opportunity, they believe, everyone must have the same chance of gaining admission, which is 100 percent if space is available, or, at worst, the same percentage for everyone if there is not enough room for all.

If open admission is used, the university has two follow-up options. One is to try to ensure that almost all students can go on to receive a diploma, if they put in at least a decent amount of effort. Because some individuals are not particularly adroit as students, such a practice generally results in a university's having rather low standards, at least for passing. The second follow-up option, used more often in Europe and especially France, is to admit all students, but then flunk out many of them. For example, in France, there are different diplomas depending on the number of years one is able to stay at the university. In this way, standards are kept high, but at the same time, large numbers of students never finish the program they intended to finish. They are left with educations that are incomplete from almost any point of view.

Open admission has not been popular in the United States except where it has been legislated. One reason may be that, at least in present times, the practice of flunking out large numbers of students is not popular. Indeed, many students seem to become distressed if they receive any grade lower than an A, and many professors have taken the path of least resistance and given grades that meet students' exceedingly high expectations.

A related reason is that, even with competitive admissions, standards for what is expected of students probably have declined over the years. Certainly, the quality and quantity of work required for an A has gone down. It has to have, with many colleges reporting A's being given to half or more of students in a particular course. Another symptom of the decline is the falling reading level of books assigned to students, a change that professors have decried (even as they clamor for lower-level books). And this happens with credentialed admissions. With open admissions, the expectation is that declines in standards would be even greater.

In addition, the United States has tended to opt for what the population perceives as a more meritocratic system, even if it is less "democratic" in the sense of everyone having an equal chance to attend any school. The problem of defining what constitutes merit has been a vexing one, but on the whole, schools have decided for a system in which grades, standardized test scores, letters of recommendation, and extracurricular activities play a major role in the admissions process. In the United States, this system has been viewed as democratic in the sense that it ideally gives each student an equal chance to succeed and thus gain college admission. In practice, probably no one believes that each student truly gets an equal opportunity to succeed. If a student grows up in an inner-city environment, the chances are that he or she will not have the same educational opportunities as a student who goes to school in a wealthy suburb. Rather, what admissions committees do is look at indicators of future success, while trying to take into account a student's background and available opportunities, and then try to select a diverse class where students will be able to do the work and contribute to the college community as a whole.

Another reason has to do with rewarding hard work. It would be hard to sell open admissions as a generalized procedure in the United States because such admissions would run contrary to the view that people should be rewarded for their efforts, or punished for not trying hard enough. If institutions were to take away the college admissions contest, then the fear is that students would have little incentive to work hard in high school.

Research in psychology, however, has shown that so-called extrinsic rewards can undermine intrinsic motivation. In other words, if one does something for the sheer pleasure of doing it, but then a system of rewards is introduced by which one is given concrete awards for doing the same things, eventually one starts doing the things not for the enjoyment of them, but for the rewards. As counterintuitive as it may seem, giving rewards can actually destroy the pleasure that people once took in doing an activity.

In the educational system of the United States, extrinsic rewards have done a fairly thorough job of undermining whatever intrinsic motivation students may have had for studying hard. With few exceptions, schools grade performance, and the grades are for high stakes. The result is that students often work for grades rather than for any joy they might otherwise experience in learning.

For all these reasons, open admissions has not caught on in the United States, except among community colleges and a few other colleges. This is a big exception, however, because large numbers of students begin their career in higher education in a community college. Many such students later transfer to four-year colleges. But because higher prestige is associated with more selective admissions, it is unlikely that the system will spread widely anytime soon.

GEOGRAPHICALLY RESTRICTED ADMISSIONS

In Spain, there are severe geographic restrictions on where students can go to universities. In general, they are expected to go to universities that reflect where in the country they live. In the United States, the system of state-supported colleges and universities is somewhat more flexible, but nevertheless enforces restrictions and, sometimes, quotas. If a student is applying to a state-sponsored university from out of state, the standards for admission are generally higher, and the possibility of matriculation is further reduced by what are usually substantially higher rates of tuition than in-state students would pay.

Because this system is so entrenched in the United States, it is rarely questioned. But it does result in imbalances of educational opportunities across the country, much as the elementary-secondary system results in imbalances when students are allowed to go only to schools in their own communities. In the case of the higher education system, a student growing up in North Dakota has an edge in admission to, say, the University of North Dakota, centered in Grand Forks. A student growing up in California has an edge in admissions at the University of California, Berkeley, one of the most prestigious institutions in the world. Students in both states compete for admission to their state universities. But their success will depend in large part on the state in which they grew up.

On its face, this system seems unfair. Why should a student growing up in Fargo, North Dakota, have less of an educational opportunity than a similarly qualified student growing up in Palo Alto, California? Traditionally, the main reason offered for this disparity is that the state government funds the state universities, so it makes sense to favor in-state applicants, whose parents' taxes pay for the schools and their upkeep.

The story has changed somewhat as state legislatures have continually decreased their contributions to the state universities. Indeed, today many state universities have to obtain the overwhelming proportion of their support from sources other than their legislatures, making them "state" universities more in name than in funding. Some universities have even talked of privatizing, although state legislatures to date have been possessive of their universities, wanting power without wanting to pay for it.

The structure of state universities is unlikely to change anytime soon, so it is likely that these universities will continue to give strong geographic preferences to residents of their own states. But then, private universities also have geographic preferences, except that they are not codified. A qualified student applying to Harvard or Yale from Montana has an edge over a qualified student from Massachusetts or Connecticut, because both universities seek geographic diversity and have a harder time attracting highly able students from Montana than from nearby their campuses. The population of Montana is relatively small, and many Montanans, for geographic, academic, or financial reasons, might not readily think of these colleges as plausible options. So whether codified or not, place of residence matters quite a bit in the United States, as it does in much of Europe.

FLEXIBLE ADMISSIONS

Most selective institutions use a system of flexible admissions. They take into account high-school GPA and standardized test scores, but interpret them in the context of the many variables that can influence them. They also take into account other factors, such as athletic, musical, artistic, and scientific accomplishments, experience in student government, and experience in other service work. And they consider letters of recommendation, application essays, and sometimes, personal interviews.

Flexible admissions may be done in the context of affirmative action, or may be blind to affirmative-action considerations. Some schools also attempt to achieve flexible admissions in a need-blind way that guarantees that financial need will not be a factor in admission. In practice, only a small number of schools are able to reach, and fewer are able to maintain, a truly need-blind admissions practice.

The system proposed in this book augments that of flexible admissions. It does not replace existing indices but rather adds new ones. It is based on the notion that current assessments tend to be narrower than they should be, and that, with broader assessments, we better can reach our goals of academic excellence coupled with diversity.

Diversity has become a source of consternation and even of apprehension among some applicants and their parents. The feeling is that a student who is a perfectly good applicant may be rejected to make room for a "diverse" applicant, whatever "diverse" is supposed to mean. The apprehension is not unfounded. As explained earlier, colleges do seek diversity and it is harder to get into Harvard if you are from New York City than if you are from Butte, Montana, and harder to get in if you don't happen to be captain of an athletic team than if you are the captain.

My wife, Karin, who is from Germany, finds all this emphasis on diversity puzzling. The school from which she graduated, the University of Heidelberg, admits students based on their school grades. Whether you are an athletic or musical superstar does not matter one whit, and any time you spent on athletics or music that took away from your school grades was at your own risk. The same is true in most of Europe and, indeed, in most of the world. Many people in the United States share Karin's puzzlement. What is the relevance of all this "diversity" stuff to college admissions?

In the election campaign between Obama and McCain, the country witnessed firsthand what happens when people are brought up lacking appreciation, or even tolerance of, diversity. The smear campaign against Obama—that he was "not like us," a closet terrorist, even the anti-Christ—was appalling, but predictable. At the same time, there were smears against McCain on account of his age. Smears have been used in U.S. political campaigns since our country was founded. What was not so predictable was the extent to which people believed what they heard. Perhaps we should have expected it, given that John Kerry, the Vietnam War hero, had been painted as a coward in an earlier election campaign against presidential and vice-presidential candidates who had not served in Vietnam.

We need diversity in our colleges and universities to teach students to understand, appreciate, and even value viewpoints other than their own. At Tufts, for example, most students are Democrats. It is important to ensure that there are Republicans in the mix so that students can come to understand how others could have points of view that are different. The same would be true of a campus composed mostly of Republicans. What went on in Alaska when it nearly reelected Senator Ted Stevens after he was convicted of multiple felonies (convictions that were later overturned)? It would help the discussion on college campuses if some students from Alaska were there who might be able to explain what people were thinking. Years ago, when O. J. Simpson was acquitted of criminal charges, the same percentage of African Americans thought he was innocent as the percentage of white Americans who thought he was guilty. In order for each group to understand the other's point of view, they needed to be able to interact. And did women, on average, view the Hillary Clinton candidacy differently than did men? If there were no women students on campus, or if there were no men, one could not find out, at least through direct dialogue.

Without diversity, the intellectual life of a campus is constricted. People may come to believe that their own point of view is the only sensible one, or even the only one. Parents sometimes fail to realize that, when they send their children away to college, they are paying as much for the fellow students their child will meet as they are for the professors and campus facilities. The fellow students will help shape the beliefs of the student and may become lifelong friends. If they all have the same point of view, the student will miss out on one of the most important aspects of a college education—learning how to understand and appreciate diverse points of view.

CHAPTER 4

A NEW WAY OF LOOKING AT

INTELLIGENCE AND SUCCESS

The greatest problem facing colleges and universities today—in their admissions, instruction, and assessment—is that many administrators are locked into an archaic notion of what it means to be intelligent. This dated notion has resulted in a tremendous waste of human resources, as well as the miseducation of millions of youngsters.

WHAT IS INTELLIGENCE?

What specifically is involved in intelligent thinking? Two symposia held in 1921 and 1986 tackled this question by trying to ascertain the key features of intelligence.[1] According to experts gathered at these symposia, the critical elements of intelligence are the abilities to (1) adapt to meet the demands of the environment, (2) engage in elementary processes of perception and attention, (3) use higher-level processes of abstract reasoning, mental representation, problem solving, and decision making, (4) learn, and (5) respond effectively to problem situations.

But the symposia's findings are just one exchange in a long and contentious debate over what comprises intelligence. Some experts, such as Edwin Boring in 1923, have been content to define intelligence operationally, that is, simply as the intelligence quotient, or IQ.[2] Originally, IQ was defined as a ratio of one's mental-age level of performance to one's chronological-age level of performance, but today IQs are computed simply in terms of how much one differs from the average. An average IQ is 100, and slightly more than two-thirds of IQs fall between 85 and 115.

Expert definitions rely on tests such as those originated by Alfred Binet and Theodore Simon in 1916 to measure judgmental abilities or of David Wechsler in 1939 to measure verbal and performance abilities.[3] Earlier tests proposed by Francis Galton in 1883 measured psychophysical abilities (such as sensitivity of hearing or touch).[4] They proved to be less valid, because they correlated neither with each other nor with success in educational settings.

The most influential theories—those that underlie IQ tests and tests such as the ACT and the SAT—are psychometric ones— theories that are based on quantitative measurements. Although tests such as the SAT and ACT claim not to be measures of intelligence, they correlate so highly with IQ tests that they are essentially interchangeable with them.[5] These tests are not the only ways in which admissions officers judge applicants' intelligence and credentials for admission, but they often form an integral part of these judgments. The psychometric theories are based on and often tested by analyses of individual differences in scores among people who take tests.

Conventional intelligence tests, which originated largely at the turn of the twentieth century, became especially popular during World War I as a means of screening soldiers. Then and now, the tests have tended, on average, to favor individuals of higher socioeconomic status and, in the United States, those who are European American or Asian American rather than African American or Hispanic American. There are many alternative explanations for these differences, but the large majority of scholars view them as being environmental in origin.

Among these theories, the earliest major one is that mentioned earlier, of Charles Spearman, who proposed that intelligence comprises a general factor *(g)* of intelligence common to all intellectual tasks, as well as specific factors *(s)*, each of which is unique to a given test of intelligence.[6] His 1927 proposal was based on his finding of a "positive manifold" among intelligence tests: all tests seemed to be positively intercorrelated, suggesting the existence of a general factor. Spearman's theory still has many proponents today, such as Arthur Robert Jensen, whose analyses of factor-analytic and other data suggest what he believes to be a single factor underlying virtually all intellectual performances.[7] Back in 1938, however, Louis Leon Thurstone disagreed with Spearman, arguing that the general factor was an artifact of the way Spearman had analyzed his data. Thurstone suggested that seven primary mental abilities underlie intelligence: verbal comprehension, verbal fluency, number skills, spatial visualization, inductive reasoning, memory, and perceptual speed.[8]

More modern theorists, such as Raymond Cattell and John Bissell Carroll, have attempted to integrate these two kinds of views, suggesting that intelligence is best understood hierarchically, with a general factor at the top of the hierarchy (that is, in a place more central to intelligence) and narrower factors under it.[9] Cattell proposed two such factors: fluid intelligence, which is involved in reasoning with novel kinds of stimuli; and crystallized intelligence, or one's stored knowledge base.

What is the purpose of all this discussion of intelligence, given that no testing organization claims that its college admissions test is an intelligence test, and admissions officers do not see the tests in this way? Because, first, the distinction between these tests is the result of a carefully planted illusion that tests like the SAT measure distinctively different knowledge and skills than those measured by conventional intelligence tests. But the evidence against such a distinction is substantial. The SAT is divided into two sections, with the morning section called a "reasoning test." Most intelligence tests are, in large part, also reasoning tests. Most theories of intelligence have reasoning at their core. Indeed, Charles Spearman's formulation of the general factor followed from his work on the qualitative and quantitative principles of reasoning.[10] In my own and others' research, it has been found that reasoning tests are highly correlated with intelligence tests because they are at the center of what intelligence tests measure.[11] Indeed, Jean Piaget made this point long before I did—that intellectual development is in large part the development of inferential reasoning processes.[12] What is often considered the most "pure" intelligence test, the Raven Progressive Matrices, is a test of inductive reasoning.

Underlying reasoning is, in part, working memory, measured both by intelligence tests and by college admissions tests, especially tests of reading comprehension.[13] The testing companies have gone out of their way not to do the obvious—to report detailed correlations between college admissions and intelligence tests. The results would most likely undermine the companies' creation of a vague but supposedly distinctly separate construct based on scores from their tests. The fact that the tests have different labels, and that people have gone to great lengths to duck their heads in the sand regarding what psychological construct these tests measure, does not change this basic fact. Moreover, tests can look very different on the surface but still measure the same construct. Different IQ tests, for example, such as the Stanford-Binet and the Wechsler, look different, but measure largely the same construct. Arthur Jensen, as well as Richard Herrnstein and Charles Murray, among others, have shown that despite all the differences in names, tests of reasoning such as the ones used in college admissions are largely intelligence tests.[14] (And indeed, one can argue that in the case of the SAT, there is no real clear name. As mentioned earlier, "SAT" was first an acronym for "Scholastic Aptitude Test," then for "Scholastic Assessment Test," and is now an acronym for nothing at all.)

The biggest problem with the psychometric theories of intelligence that dominate our thinking is that they put the cart before the horse. Basically, investigators looked for tests that would predict school achievement, then declared those tests to be tests of "intelligence." Because Binet's job was to predict school performance, it is understandable that the roots of current testing would be tests that predict academic performance (as well as, to a lesser degree, job performance). But we do not have to look far to discover that the folk conception, or "implicit theory," of intelligence as performance on highly structured academic tests is limited both by space (culture) and time (era)—for intelligence may be conceived in different ways in different cultures and by different generations. In an increasingly interactive world, we clearly need to view our policies in light of modern, global considerations. More and more students who are being admitted to universities are international students, and even American students from diverse cultural backgrounds may look at intelligence in a wide variety of ways.

INTELLIGENCE ACROSS CULTURES

Conceptions of intelligence seem to vary widely across cultures. Contemporary Taiwanese Chinese conceptions of intelligence, for example, span five areas: (1) a general cognitive factor, much like the g factor in conventional Western tests, (2) interpersonal intelligence (social competence), (3) intrapersonal intelligence (understanding oneself), (4) intellectual self-assertion—knowing when to show you are smart, and (5) intellectual self-effacement—knowing when not to show you are smart.[15] By contrast, my colleagues and I have found that Americans' conceptions of intelligence center on three areas: practical problem solving, verbal ability, and social competence. In both the Taiwanese and American cases, however, people's implicit theories of intelligence seem to extend beyond what conventional psychometric intelligence tests measure.[16]

Studies in Africa in fact provide yet another window on the substantial differences across cultures. Patricia Ruzgis and Elena Grigorenko have argued that, in Africa, conceptions of intelligence revolve largely around skills that help to facilitate and maintain harmonious and stable intergroup relations; intragroup relations, too, are probably equally important and at times more important.[17] Robert Serpell has found that Chewa adults in Zambia emphasize social responsibilities, cooperativeness, and obedience as important to intelligence; intelligent students are expected to be respectful of adults.[18] Charles Super and Sara Harkness have found that Kenyan parents also emphasize responsible participation in family and social life as important aspects of intelligence.[19] In Zimbabwe, the word for intelligence, *ngware*, actually means to be prudent and cautious, particularly in social relationships. And among the Baoulé people of Ghana and Côte d'Ivoire, service to the family and community, as well as politeness toward and respect for elders, is seen as key to intelligence.[20]

The emphasis on the social aspects of intelligence is not limited to African cultures. Notions of intelligence in many Asian cultures also emphasize the social aspect of intelligence more than does the conventional Western or IQ-based idea. But even as the African and Asian cultures emphasize social skills in their definitions of intelligence more than the U.S. culture does, they also recognize the importance of cognitive aspects of intelligence. In a study of Kenyan conceptions of intelligence, for example, it was found that there are four distinct terms constituting conceptions of intelligence among rural Kenyans—*rieko* (knowledge and skills), *luoro* (respect), *winjo* (comprehension of how to handle real-life problems), and *paro* (initiative). Note that only the first of these refers directly to knowledge-based skills, of which academic skills are just a part.[21]

But remember too that there is no one overall U.S. conception of intelligence. Indeed, one study found that various ethnic groups in San Jose, California, had rather different ideas about what it means to be intelligent.[22] For example, Latino parents of students tended to emphasize the importance of social-competence skills in their conceptions of intelligence, whereas Asian and Anglo parents tended to emphasize the significance of cognitive skills. Teachers, who were often of Anglo background, also emphasized cognitive skills over social competence. The rank order of performance of students of various groups (including subgroups within the Latino and Asian groups) could be perfectly predicted by the extent to which their parents shared the teachers' conception of intelligence. In other words, teachers tended to reward those students who were socialized into a view of intelligence that happened to correspond to the teachers' own.

Similarly, when teachers write letters of recommendation for applicants to college, they apply their implicit theories of intelligence, so much so that the letters reflect these implicit theories as much as anything about the applicants themselves. But even if teachers do not reward social aspects of intelligence as much as the cognitive aspects, these social aspects may be as important as the cognitive, or even more so, to one's success in later life.

In traditional admissions, certain groups tend to perform less well on traditional admission tests than do other groups. And the usual response has been to throw up one's hands and conclude that a merit-based system will not work, because it will always disfavor members of groups that affirmative action is intended to serve. But we have given up too easily. A merit-based system is both possible and feasible.

SUCCESSFUL INTELLIGENCE DEFINED

The system I advocate here is based on my psychological theory of abilities, called the augmented theory of successful intelligence.[23] Successful intelligence is the ability to succeed in life. People have different conceptions of success (for example, to be a successful scientist, athlete, actor, musician, writer, accountant, plumber, secretary, business executive), and a conception of intelligence needs to take into account that people work toward diverse goals and do so within different cultural milieus.

Successful intelligence involves three components of intelligence: analytical, creative, and practical. Analytical intelligence is what traditional IQ tests and SATs measure. Creative intelligence involves going beyond the given, and thinking flexibly and adaptively in rapidly changing situations. And practical intelligence is the use of one's abilities to make a difference in one's everyday life.

In the everyday world, people are not smart merely in one way or another. That is, they are not merely adept in an analytical way, highly creative, or savvy in a practical intelligence sense—or none of the above. There is a continuum of levels of skill in each of these domains. So one person might rank fairly high in analytical ability, even higher in creative skill, and low in practical savoir faire, or another might have excellent analytical abilities but struggle in areas involving creative or practical skill. There is some correlation among the abilities because they are not completely independent.[24] For example, a successful creative person needs not only to come up with novel ideas, but also analytically to assess which ideas are best as well as practically to figure out how to persuade others to accept them.

THE TACIT DIMENSION OF SUCCESSFUL INTELLIGENCE

Significantly, practical intelligence draws largely on tacit knowledge.[25] Tacit knowledge is viewed as knowledge that generally is acquired with little support from other people or resources. In other words, the individual is not directly instructed as to what he or she should learn, but rather must extract the important lessons from experience even when learning is not the primary objective.

Because tacit knowledge is an understanding of how to perform various tasks in different situations, it can be considered a subset of procedural knowledge that is drawn from personal experience. And as is the case with much procedural knowledge, it tends to guide action without being easily articulated. That is, when it comes to tacit knowledge, we often do not know what we know.

Part of the difficulty in articulating tacit knowledge is that it typically reflects a set of complex, multiconditional rules for how to pursue particular goals in specific situations (for example, rules about how to judge people accurately for a variety of purposes and under a range of circumstances). These complex rules can be represented in the form of condition-action (or "if-then") pairings. For example, knowledge about confronting one's superior might be represented like so:

IF <you are in a public forum>
AND
IF <the boss says something or does something that you perceive is wrong or inappropriate>
AND
IF <the boss does not ask for questions or comments>
THEN <speak directly to the point of contention and do not make evaluative statements about your boss>
BECAUSE <this saves the boss from embarrassment and preserves your relationship with him>.

In other words, tacit knowledge is more than a set of abstract procedural rules. It is context-specific knowledge about what to do in a given situation or kind of situation.

An additional characteristic feature of tacit knowledge is that it has direct relevance to the individual's goals. Knowledge that is based on one's own practical experience probably will be more instrumental to achieving one's goals than knowledge that is generic or based on someone else's experience. For example, leaders may be taught which leadership approach (say, authoritative or participative) is supposed to be most appropriate in a given situation, but they may learn from their own experiences that some other strategy will be more effective.

Consider a study we did in rural Usenge, Kenya, that investigated tacit knowledge in rural Kenyan children.[26] To learn about school-age students' ability to adapt to their indigenous environment, we devised a test of practical intelligence. This test measured students' informal, tacit knowledge about natural herbal medicines that the villagers believe are effective against various types of infections. More than 95 percent of the students in the villages suffer from parasitic illnesses, and they use their knowledge of these medicines an average of once a week in medicating themselves and others. The students' well-being depends on their being able to self-medicate; those who cannot self-medicate will suffer more from the parasitic illnesses. But this is clearly not a kind of knowledge that is important across all cultures. Middle-class Westerners who have no idea about these herbal medicines would probably find it challenging to thrive or even survive in these contexts (or, for that matter, in the U.S. urban ghettos often not distant from their comfortable homes).

We measured the Kenyan students' ability to identify the natural herbal medicines by where they come from, what they are used for, and what doses are appropriate. Based on work that we had done elsewhere, we expected that scores on this test would not correlate with scores on conventional tests of intelligence. In order to test this hypothesis, we also administered to the eighty-five students the Raven Coloured Progressive Matrices Test, which is a measure of fluid or abstract-reasoning-based abilities, as well as the Mill Hill Vocabulary Scale, which assesses crystallized or formal-knowledge-based abilities. In addition, we gave the students a comparable test of vocabulary in their own Dholuo language. The Dholuo language is spoken in the home, whereas English is used in the schools.

The results we encountered were suprising in terms of traditional theories of human intelligence. To our surprise, we found statistically significant correlations of the tacit-knowledge tests with the tests of crystallized abilities. The correlations, however, were negative. In other words, the higher the students scored on the test of tacit knowledge, the lower they scored, on average, on the tests of crystallized abilities. Tests of fluid abilities also showed correlations with practical intelligence in the negative direction.

These surprising results can be interpreted in various ways, but based on the ethnographic observations of the anthropologists on the team, we concluded that a plausible scenario would include families' expectations for their students. Many students drop out of school before graduation for financial or other reasons. Moreover, many families in the village do not particularly value formal Western schooling. There is no reason they should, because the students of many families will spend their lives farming or engaged in other occupations that make little or no use of Western schooling. Few if any will go to universities. Instead, then, the families emphasize teaching their students what they need to know to successfully adapt to the environments in which they will really live. Students who spend their time learning this indigenous practical knowledge of the community generally do not invest themselves heavily in doing well in school, whereas students who do well in school generally do not invest themselves as heavily in learning the indigenous knowledge—hence the negative correlations. In fact, in some cases the students who are most successful at school do not learn the indigenous knowledge because no one wants to teach them—that is, they may be perceived as the "losers" in the village.

The Kenya study suggests that the identification of a general factor of human intelligence on conventional tests, including those for college admission, may tell us more about how well an applicant's abilities match up with expectations from schools, especially schools based on Western patterns of education, than it does about his or her ability to succeed in life.

Further, our research shows that the context-specificity of intellectual performance applies not only to countries far removed from North America or Europe. One can find the same on these continents, as we did in our study of Yup'ik Eskimo students in southwestern Alaska.[27]

We were particularly interested in these students because their teachers thought that, for the most part, they lacked even the basic intelligence needed for success in school. Yet many of the students had tremendous practical knowledge that few, if any, of the teachers had. For example, the Yup'ik students could travel easily from one village to another in the winter on a dogsled because they had the ability to recognize even the most subtle landmarks in the frozen tundra. The outsider teachers (and we the researchers), had we tried to do the same, most likely would have died after becoming lost in those same hundreds of miles of seemingly barren landscape.

My collaborators and I decided to compare the importance of academic and practical intelligence among rural and urban Alaskan communities. A total of 261 students were rated for practical skills by adults or peers in the study as well as by a test of tacit (informally learned) knowledge as acquired in rural Alaskan Yup'ik communities, and we measured academic intelligence with conventional measures of fluid and crystallized intelligence. Tests of fluid intelligence measured abstract-reasoning skills and tests of crystallized intelligence measured world knowledge, such as vocabulary.

The urban students generally outperformed the rural students on a measure of crystallized intelligence, but the rural students generally outperformed the urban students on the measure of Yup'ik tacit knowledge. The test of tacit knowledge was superior to the tests of academic intelligence in predicting practical and, particularly, hunting skills of the rural students (for whom the test was created), but not of the urban students. Thus in terms of the skills that mattered most to the students' everyday lives, such as staying alive in a challenging environment, the test of practical intelligence was the way to go.

I live in the West End of Boston. Students growing up in the largely middle-class area in which I live, or in wealthy suburbs such as Weston or Wellesley, will have had many opportunities to learn the academic skills that conventional tests value. They have a distinct edge in getting into the college or university of their choice, affirmative action notwithstanding. Just a few miles from where I live is Roxbury, the most economically challenged part of Boston and one with a relatively high crime rate. So what kinds of skills do these students develop? Actually, quite a few, but not necessarily the skills measured by tests such as the SAT or the ACT. Like the Yup'ik Eskimo students, they develop skills that are exquisitely adapted to the environments in which they live. Some of them have to get between their home and school in the face of potential violence and other threats to their safety. They have to learn to deal with, and hopefully not become, drug dealers. They have to live with families that may be in disarray, in part as a result of economic and social challenges. How many of us comfortably could walk those streets, especially in the dark, and make it from point A to point B safely? How many of us would even try? Actually, some of us may end up having to learn. Recent upheavals in the society as a whole may encourage the development of a broader range of skills among students who move from the middle class to lower social classes as their parents lose their jobs and perhaps even their homes.

Students learn the skills they need to adapt. What we should be measuring is their ability to pick up adaptive skills, not merely their ability to pick up skills that happen to be on the tests.

SUCCESSFUL INTELLIGENCE AND STANDARDIZED TESTS

One could argue that standardized tests like the SAT and ACT are not supposed to tell us anything about the broader structure of human abilities. Instead, what the testing companies do purport to evaluate with their admissions tests are academic skills. This focus is largely a marketing decision, and a reasonable one, given the companies' and colleges' shared goals. It would be counterproductive to both their goals, given the current times, to label the tests "intelligence tests." But statistically, conventional intelligence is largely what the tests measure. Verbal comprehension and reasoning (measured in verbal reasoning sections), mathematical/numerical skills (measured in mathematical reasoning sections), and verbal fluency (measured in writing sections) are factors that come directly out of Thurstone's, Guilford's, and

other scholars' theories of intelligence. Call them what you will—
these categories are integral to traditional psychometric theories
of intelligence.[28]

Throughout history and in many places still, schooling, especially for boys, takes the form of apprenticeships in which students learn a craft from an early age. The students are taught
what they will need to know in order to succeed in a trade, but
not a lot more. They are not simultaneously engaged in tasks that
foster the development of the particular blend of skills measured
by conventional intelligence tests. In particular, they do not typically study a variety of subjects from an early age as Western
schoolchildren do, and because traditional intelligence tests typically measure skills in a variety of areas, they are thus at a disadvantage. Even more to the point, it is less likely that one would
observe a "general intelligence factor" in their scores. Our research in Kenya bears out this assertion.

One might wonder what a study done in rural Kenya has to
do with students in the United States, particularly those in urban
settings. Actually, it has everything to do with them. Most students do not want to become academic superstars who later become professors to the next generation of academic superstars.
Rather, they have a wide variety of goals in life. If a student
wants to become an NBA superstar, an actor, a dancer, a violinist, an artist, or involved in any of a number of other occupations, it is not clear that getting into Harvard and then getting A's
in an academically challenging major such as physics is the right
way to get there. In fact, going to Harvard and excelling academically may be precisely the wrong step. A ballet dancer has relatively little time in which to make his or her name, and generally
cannot afford to take off four years to study academic pursuits.
A potential NBA or NFL star will not get the kind of athletic
training at Harvard that will propel him into the elite world of
professional basketball or football. A violinist needs to spend
countless hours practicing—not cramming for difficult exams—
and unless he or she spends much of the time in deliberate prac-

tice, hopes of a professional career, particularly as a soloist, may go out the window.

In some jobs, the credential will make a difference for entrance. For example, some top investment banks or law firms will recruit only at the more prestigious colleges and universities. These cases point out that, to some extent, higher education has become a business of buying a credential in addition to an education. But although the origin of the credential may matter a great deal for initial placement, it will probably matter less for promotion, including to top management, legal, or other positions. At that point, it will be the actual education one received that matters rather than merely the name of one's alma mater.

Even as basic a skill as memory, which schools emphasize and which admissions tests measure, can develop differently in various cultures. One investigator asked Moroccan and North American individuals to remember patterns of Oriental rugs as well as pictures of everyday objects such as a rooster and a fish. In short, the Moroccans in the study, whose culture has traditionally involved experience in the rug trade, seemed to remember things in a different way from participants who did not have their skill in remembering rug patterns, and they were better at remembering those patterns.[29] In a related study, Judith Kearins found that when asked to remember visuospatial displays, Anglo Australians used verbal (school-appropriate) strategies whereas aboriginals used visual strategies appropriate to their desert-nomad culture.[30] Thus, students may develop different skills, or apply the same skills differently, as a function of their cultural background.

PRACTICAL KNOWLEDGE IN ACTION

Consider another example. A young man whom I'll call Adam was in a great business school. As an MBA student, he could expect a very bright future. While a student, he started a business that proved to be very successful. As Adam progressed through school, he spent more and more time on the business and less and less time on his schoolwork. His grades, which were high at first, started to show where he was putting his time. The more successful the business became, the more his grades suffered. Then Adam was offered funding by a major venture-capital firm, but with the stipulation that he become a full-time CEO of the business. So there he was, in the position of a rural Kenyan schoolchild. He could spend his time on his courses in business school and neglect what he felt he needed to do to succeed in the real world, or he could let the academic work go. He let the academic work go and eventually dropped out of business school with only months left to go. The gamble paid off, and the business thrived beyond what anyone originally might have hoped. For this entrepreneur, academic development and success in the world of work had developed a negative correlation, and Adam chose the world of work, much as did the practically more successful students in rural Kenya. But he took a risk: if the business had failed, he might well have ended up back in business school.

Awhile back, I attended the commencement ceremony for Tufts University. The commencement speaker was Michael Bloomberg, the mayor of New York. He commented that he was pleased to be back in Medford, Massachusetts, where he grew up. He congratulated the president of the university on being first in his class, and then commented on how he, Bloomberg, was one of those who made the top half of the class possible. The audience laughed. Underlying the humor, however, was a serious message: success in life does not necessarily originate with academic success.

I used to spend a lot of my time fund-raising. Fund-raising involved meeting some of the most successful alumni of Tufts, as measured not only by their financial resources and, hence, giving capacity, but also by the contributions they have made to society. Many of the people I met were in business, but certainly not all or even almost all. One thing impressed me, as I am sure it has countless other deans and other fund-raisers in the past: many of the people with whom I met were not at the top of their class at Tufts, nor were they admitted with sky-high GPAs or SATs. Sometimes they had comparatively lackluster academic records upon admission, and often their academic records upon graduation were not much better. But many of them developed other practical skills that had enabled them to make a significant difference to the world with whatever resources were available to them.

When we admit students to colleges, one question we have to ask ourselves is why academic skill is as important as we make it out to be. If college grades are so important to success, why are top graduates thirty years later often not those who received the highest academic honors? According to the theory of successful intelligence, people succeed by capitalizing on strengths and by compensating for or correcting their weaknesses. There is no one formula for success. Everyone has to find his or her own, based on a unique pattern of strengths and weaknesses. This postulate, in turn, implies that abilities can be changed—that people can indeed correct their weaknesses if they set their sights on doing so.

Consider the best teachers you have ever had, and then ask yourself what made them so good. Chances are that they were great teachers in different ways. One teacher may have excelled in lecturing to large classes, another in leading seminars, another in mentoring one on one. Similarly, CEOs have different styles, but all can succeed if they find a fit between their style and the company they lead. In the end, no one is good at everything, and no one is bad at everything. People who are successfully intelligent are those who figure out their strengths and find a way to capitalize on them. People who are less successfully intelligent either never figure out what they do well, or, having figured it out, fail to find a way to make the most of it.

It is also important as well to figure out how to compensate for or correct weaknesses. Bill Clinton had the potential to be a president of historical proportions. Educated at Georgetown and Yale Law School, he was universally agreed to have a combination of intellectual brilliance, gregariousness, and personal charisma that are rarely found in politicians at any level. He also had a weakness, which was an inability to resist extramarital adventures with women. For whatever reason, he was unable to correct this weakness during his leadership years, and ended up paying a steep price for it. So did the country, as Clinton spent more and more of his time enmeshed in scandal. As went Bill Clinton, so went John Edwards and Mark Sanford, two other brilliant politicians whose careers went down the tubes as a result of their sexual escapades. Similarly, George Bush had an education most people can only dream about: Phillips Andover Academy, followed by Yale and then Harvard Business School. Yet the greatest financial crisis since the Great Depression began on his watch, as did other serious problems, such as the scandal at the Abu Ghraib prison in Iraq. Although there are many reasons for these errors, one almost certainly was Bush's periodic difficulty in learning from mistakes. Even many Republicans, toward the end of his term, were discouraged by his emphasis on big government and federal centralization. And his ability to anticipate reactions to his policies, domestically and abroad, bordered on the tone deaf. In the end, two presidents in a row with terrific educations proved to be surprisingly challenged leaders. Both had weaknesses, and neither figured out a way adequately to correct or compensate for these weaknesses.

All of us have weaknesses. For one person, it may be a bad temper or a tendency to shoot from the hip. I was once a consultant to a very successful executive who tended to be impulsive in his responses to bad news. At one point, he received a phone call telling him that he had been passed over for a promotion. His reaction was to explode and explain to his boss why the person who was moving up was a poor choice and why he would have been a better one. In the end, he not only lost a challenging job opportunity, but his job as well. His one notable weakness proved to be his downfall.

In college admissions, we seek not only well-rounded individuals who will be good at lots of things, but also young people with unusual strengths—in music, athletics, entrepreneurship, political work, acting, or whatever—and, moreover, the ability to capitalize on these strengths. In the end, those who can capitalize on a few strengths and compensate for (or remedy) their weaknesses will be those who achieve the greatest success.

It can be difficult for college admissions officers to pick up on which students will capitalize on strengths and compensate or correct for weaknesses. But there are ways to increase the probability of identifying such tendencies. One is to give applicants a variety of opportunities to show how they stand out. Even the very process of giving applicants multiple options will reveal whether they can figure out how to demonstrate their strengths. Moreover, if admissions officers do interviews, they can ask students about not only their strengths but also their weaknesses and how they deal with those weaknesses. The information provided will be tainted a bit by the student's desire to look good, of course, but such questions can still provide insights useful to the college admissions process.

These principles apply to us all, including me. I was until recently dean of the School of Arts and Sciences at Tufts. One of my strengths, I believed, was that I came from outside the university. This outsider background enabled me to see opportunities for improvement that colleagues who had been at Tufts longer were unable to see. In any organization, people get used to the way things are, and can have trouble recognizing how things could be another way. But at the same time, and more unexpectedly, my outsider status was a weakness: because I was new to Tufts, I only had a rough idea of how things were done there. My solution? When openings for academic deanships arose, I chose insiders to fill them—people who had been at Tufts for a long time. And as I predicted, they did, on any number of occasions, save me from myself, preventing me from making mistakes that might have occurred because I did not yet fully understand the organizational culture.

CREATIVITY: STORIES FROM THE FIELD

While I was teaching at Yale, three graduate students with whom I worked provided a curious contrast in the types of skills that accompany—or fail to accompany—what we call intelligence. The first, whom I have come to call Alice, was brilliant academically and at the kinds of memory and analytical skills that conventional psychometric tests of intelligence emphasize. She started off our graduate program in psychology as one of the top students, but by the end of the program ranked near the bottom. The reason was transparent: Alice was brilliant analytically, but showed only the most minimal creative skills. I was not convinced that Alice was born creatively impaired. Rather, it seemed more likely that Alice had been so overly reinforced for her school smarts that she had never had any incentive to develop or even to find whatever creative skills may have lay latent in her.

Another graduate student in our program, "Celia," was admitted not because she was spectacular, but because she appeared to have strengths in both analytical and creative areas. But Celia surprised us when, upon graduation, she was besieged with job offers. It turns out that she was the kind of person who could go into a job interview, figure out what her potential employers wanted to hear, and then give it to them. In contrast, "Paul," a student who was analytically and creatively brilliant, received many job interviews but only one very lukewarm job offer after managing to insult his interviewers at every turn. He was as low in practical intelligence as Celia was adept in this very important area.

Still another student, "Barbara," was marvelously creative, if we were to believe her portfolio of research work and the recommendations of her undergraduate professors, but her scores on the largely analytical Graduate Record Examination (GRE) were weak. Barbara was rejected from our program, but I hired her as a research associate, which gave her a chance to show her creative brilliance. Barbara was admitted as the top pick to our graduate program a couple of years later. Some years later, we did a study on twelve years of graduate students in psychology at Yale. The study showed that, although the GRE was a good predictor of first-year grades, it was a satisfactory predictor of little else, such as students' analytical, creative, practical, research, or teaching abilities, or the quality of their dissertation.[31] For men, the analytical section (since discontinued) had some predictive power for these other criteria; for women, none of the sections had significant predictive power.

Creativity is hard to sell in some schools. Here another true-life story comes to mind, although in this case the student is much younger. "Julia" was a student in a public school comprised of largely middle-class students. Her elementary school teacher was doing a unit on the planets. To acquaint students with the planet Mars, the teacher asked the class to imagine themselves as astronauts. They were to dress up as astronauts and decide what they would do when they landed on Mars.

Julia raised her hand to make a suggestion: what if she dressed up as a Martian and greeted the astronauts when they arrived on Mars? The teacher immediately nixed Julia's idea, explaining that because it was known from space probes that there are no residents on Mars, it would not be appropriate for Julia to dress up as a Martian for the lesson.

When I heard about this incident, I was distressed. The teacher was certainly within her rights to reply as she did. But how many times do students have creative ideas, state them, and immediately get punished for doing so? And what is the lesson they learn from this kind of experience? They probably learn that the next time they have a creative idea, they should keep it to themselves. But surely this is not the lesson educators want students to learn.

The teacher's behavior was understandable and no doubt well intentioned. For one thing, there probably are no Martians (although, for a variety of reasons, that is not certain—they might live underground; they might be sending false feedback to space probes; they might be a life form that the space probes cannot recognize; and so on). And the teacher, like all teachers, probably had a staggering amount of material she was trying to cover during the term, an important consideration especially when her students' performance on statewide examinations was at stake. Yet few teacher actions kill creativity more effectively than discouraging creative ideas when they are proposed.

The stories of Barbara and Julia help us understand why it is so hard to sell creativity, both in instruction and admissions. We are a society that claims to value creativity, but we do not "walk the walk" when it comes to supporting it. The College Board added a writing test to the SAT, but its scoring is formulaic and it largely rewards cookie-cutter essays rather than creative ones. Creativity is outside the scope of the test and of what many teachers look for.

Indeed, some teachers may be put off by creativity. After all, creativity can be threatening. Although teachers probably know more facts than students and probably have more traditional academic skills at their disposal, they may not be more creative. Indeed, they may be entrenched in their thinking and, as a result, less creative. They therefore may see creative students as a threat to their self-esteem. Students may also threaten teachers' sense of control. Creative students defy the crowd, and classroom discipline is about conforming to the crowd. Teachers may thus mistake creativity for disruptiveness.

Many teachers and administrators also are unconvinced of the importance of creative thinking; they see creativity as a byproduct rather than a product of an education whose purpose, they believe, is teaching content within disciplines. Learning to engage in critical or creative thinking is often viewed as a highly peripheral add-on.

Finally, many teachers believe that creativity simply cannot be taught, even though we who study intelligence know that it can indeed be developed.[32] Teachers may view creativity as a fixed, inherited trait, and hence believe that there is little they can do to influence it.

The very nature of creativity can help fuel these misunderstandings. Creativity is notoriously difficult to measure adequately through multiple-choice or similar tests that insist on "right" or "wrong" answers. Homework, too, can be an issue: creative students may have trouble with assignments that require narrow, hard-and-fast responses. Not surprisingly, many teachers are uncomfortable with rewarding creative students whose answers fall outside of objective standards of assessment.

WISDOM: AN ESSENTIAL, AUGMENTED PART OF SUCCESSFUL INTELLIGENCE

In recent years, I have added wisdom to my theory of successful intelligence.[33] Wisdom is defined as the application of knowledge, successful intelligence, and creativity toward the achievement of a common good through a balance among intrapersonal, interpersonal, and extrapersonal interests, over the short and long terms, through the infusion of positive ethical values.[34] That is, wisdom is the skill of using one's intelligence, as well as one's knowledge, for a common good, today and long into the future.

Why is wisdom so important? Just consider what can happen when great intelligence is not accompanied by wisdom. Hitler, Stalin, and many other crackpot despots have shown how different intelligence and wisdom can be. Contemporary terrorists provide a further example. They may have the creative intelligence to select unexpected targets, the analytical intelligence to decide if they are good targets, and the practical intelligence to deliver their attacks. But they are not wise. On a more global scale, technology has progressed at a much more rapid rate than people's ability to use that technology wisely. The world has available to it enormously destructive weapons without the wisdom to know how to control or get rid of them. It is probably not an exaggeration to say that human life on the planet is at grave risk for annihilation, whether by nuclear, biological, or chemical weapons. Some leaders may think that they can use such weapons in a contained way. I am doubtful. If we do not develop greater wisdom soon, we—humankind—may never get the chance.

The difference between more and less wise thinking can be seen all around us, including in corporate America. Take just one example from the pharmaceutical company Merck. Under the leadership of former CEO Roy Vagelos, the company prospered and acquired an excellent reputation, in large part because of Vagelos's intelligent and wise decision making around a single issue, Mectizan.

Mectizan is a drug developed by scientists at Merck that combats river blindness. It thus had the potential to cure tens of thousands of individuals afflicted with this debilitating disease. The problem was that the people who needed the drug could not afford it. Many of Vagelos's advisers advised him to halt development of the drug because it was a sure money loser. Despite this advice, Vagelos decided to develop the drug and then to give it away—for free. The result was a flood of positive publicity for Merck. After Mectizan was distributed—at a loss—Merck's financial bottom line actually improved. Good leadership, characterized by good decision making, had helped the company prosper.

Years later, the same company was faced with a different challenge under former CEO Ray Gilmartin. A blockbuster drug, Vioxx, was not looking good in clinical trials. Although it was effective at reducing pain associated with arthritis, it also seemed to be associated with risk of heart damage, particularly in people who had had heart problems in the past. Under Gilmartin, Merck chose to suppress and, in some cases, "reinterpret" the results of these clinical trials. The long-term result was roughly thirty thousand lawsuits against Merck, and a company seriously damaged both financially and morally. Do more college faculty today teach one to think like Vagelos, or like Gilmartin? In more recent times, the automobile maker Toyota discovered the error of its ways in neglecting reports of sudden acceleration and failed braking in some of its cars. The damage to its reputation as well as its bottom line has been incalculable. More important, people appear to have died as a result of their Toyota-made automobiles' failures.

As defined earlier, wisdom is not just about maximizing one's own or someone else's self-interest, but also about balancing those interests with other "extrapersonal" aspects of the context in which one lives, such as one's city, country, environment, or even God. Wisdom also involves creativity, in that the wise solution to a problem may be far from obvious.

If one is wise, one certainly may seek good ends for oneself, but also must seek good outcomes for others. If one's motivations are to maximize certain people's interests and minimize other people's, wisdom is not involved—although a wise decision may lead to a common good that is better for some than for others. Consequently an evil genius may be academically intelligent and practically intelligent, but he cannot be considered wise.

Measuring an Applicant's Wisdom

One might ask whether it is possible to measure wisdom-related skills in the seventeen-year-olds who apply for college. Karin Sternberg and I have designed an assessment that measures these kinds of skills. Here is an example of the kind of problem that appears on it:

A good friend of yours seems upset. You ask him why. He then confesses to you that he is using an illegal drug. He has hidden his drug use well: To your knowledge, he showed no obvious symptoms, and no one, to your knowledge, is talking about it. His concern is not with the effects of the drug, but rather with being found out. Nevertheless, he plans to continue using the drug. He assures you that he is not addicted. He seeks advice on how to hide his stash so that no one will discover it. Moreover, he asks you not to betray his confidence. What should you do?

Answers are scored not by their exact content, but by the extent to which they seek a common good by balancing one's own, others', and larger interests, over the short and long terms, through an infusion of positive ethical values—that is, by the wisdom shown in the process of producing a response.

Ethics, Wisdom, and Learning to Stand Up

"I am very proud of myself," I told the seventeen students in a seminar I once was teaching on leadership. I had just returned from a trip, I told them, and felt that the honorarium I was paid for my consulting on ethical leadership was less than I deserved. I felt bad that I had decided to accept such a consulting engagement for so little compensation. I then told the class that I was about to fill out the reimbursement forms when I discovered that I could actually get reimbursed twice. The first reimbursement would come from the organization that had invited me, which required me merely to fill out a form listing my expenses. The second reimbursement would come from my university, which required me to submit the receipts from the trip. I explained to the class that I had worked really hard on the trip consulting about ethical leadership, and so I was pleased that by getting re-imbursed twice, I could justify to myself the amount of work I had put into the trip.

I waited for the firestorm. Would the class—which had al-ready studied leadership for several months—rise up in a mass protest against what I had done? Or would only a half-dozen brave souls raise their hands and roundly criticize me for what was obviously patently unethical behavior? I waited, and waited, and waited. Nothing happened. I then decided to move on to the main topic of the day, which, I recall, was ethical leadership. All the time I was speaking about that main topic, I expected some of the students to raise their hands and demand to return to the topic of my double reimbursement. It didn't happen.

Finally, I stopped talking about whatever the topic was, and flat-out asked the class whether any of them thought there was something off the mark with my so-called plan to obtain double reimbursement, which of course I would never really seek. If so, I told them, why had no one challenged me? I figured that, to a person, they would be embarrassed for not having challenged me. Quite a few of them were embarrassed. Others thought I must have been kidding. Still others thought that because I was the professor and a dean to boot, whatever I did I must have had a good reason for. What I did not expect, though—especially after having taught these students for several months about ethical leadership—was that some of them would commend me on my clever idea and argue that, if I could get away with it, I was entitled to receive the money—more power to me.

This experience reminded me of how hard it is to translate theories of ethics, and even case studies, into one's own practice. The students had read about ethics in leadership, heard about ethics in leadership from a variety of real-world leaders, discussed ethics in leadership, and then apparently totally failed to recognize unethical behavior when it stared them in the face. Moreover, these were students who by conventional definitions would be classified as gifted. Why is it so hard to translate theory into practice, even after one has studied ethical leadership for several months?

The problem with my students reminded me of the research on bystander intervention by Bibb Latané and John Darley.[35] They showed that, contrary to expectations, bystanders intervene when someone is in trouble only in very limited circumstances. For example, if they think that someone else might intervene, the bystanders tend to stay out of the situation. Latané and Darley even showed that divinity students who were about to lecture on the parable of the Good Samaritan were no more likely than other bystanders to help a person in distress who was in need of—a Good Samaritan.

It seems that it is far more difficult to respond ethically in real-world situations than one would expect simply on the basis of what we learn from our parents, from school, and from our religious training.

Eight Steps to Ethical Behavior

Ethical behavior involves multiple, largely sequential, steps—and unless all of the steps are completed, individuals are not likely to behave in an ethical way, regardless of the amount of training they have received in ethics, and regardless of their other skills.[36] To behave ethically, the individual has to:

1. recognize that there is an event to which to react;
2. define the event as having an ethical dimension;
3. decide that the ethical dimension is of sufficient significance to merit an ethics-guided response;
4. take personal responsibility for generating an ethical solution to the problem;
5. figure out what abstract ethical rules might apply to the problem;
6. decide how these abstract ethical rules actually apply to the problem so as to suggest a concrete solution;
7. prepare for later possible repercussions of having acted in what one considers an ethical manner; and
8. enact the ethical solution.

Seen from this standpoint, it is rather challenging to respond to problems in an ethical way. Consider the example of the supposed double reimbursement.

1. Recognize that there is an event to which to react. The students were sitting in a class on leadership, expecting to be educated by a leadership expert. In this case, I did not present the problem as one to which I expected them to react. I was simply telling them about something I had done. They had no expectation that what I, the authority figure, said would require any particular kind of reaction, except perhaps for taking notes. So for some students, the whole narrative may have been a nonevent.

This problem of not recognizing that a situation is important extends beyond this mere classroom example. When people hear their political, educational, or religious leaders talk, they may not believe there is any reason to question what they hear. After all, they are listening to authority figures. In this way, leaders, including cynical and corrupt leaders, may lead their flocks to accept and even commit unethical acts.

2. Define the event as having an ethical dimension. Not all students in the class defined the problem as an ethical one. It became clear during our later discussion that some students viewed the problem in a utilitarian way: I had worked hard, had been underpaid, and was trying to figure out a way to attain adequate compensation for my hard work. In this definition of the problem, I had come up with a clever way to make the compensation better fit the work I had done.

Cynical leaders may flaunt their unethical behavior—one is reminded today of Robert Mugabe, but there are other world leaders who might equally be relevant here. When Mugabe and his henchmen seized the property of white farmers, the seizure was presented as one of compensating alleged war heroes for their accomplishments. Why should it be unethical to compensate war heroes?

In recent times, the Chinese government apparently attempted to manipulate the media to downplay the huge ethical dimensions of an important national event.[37] On May 12, 2008, an earthquake in Sichuan province killed an estimated ten thousand schoolchildren. But there was an irregularity in the buildings that imploded during the earthquake. Schools for children of well-connected party leaders as well as government buildings withstood the earthquake with no problem. In contrast, schools housing poor children crumbled to dust. It turned out that the ill-fated schools had been built in ways that could only poorly withstand an earthquake. Presumably, the money that was supposed to have supported better construction went to line the pockets of Communist Party functionaries. The government did what it could to suppress these basic facts.

Lest one believe that only other governments attempt to obscure the ethical dimensions of events, Scott McClellan, former press secretary to President George W. Bush, claimed in a best-selling book that the president's administration engaged in many half-truths and outright lies.[38] His account suggests that members of the administration may have been unable to distinguish their lies from the truth, or may not have cared.

3. Decide that the ethical dimension is of sufficient significance to merit an ethics-guided response. In the case of my having sought double reimbursement, some of the students may have felt it was sketchy or dubious, but not sufficiently so to make an issue of it. Perhaps they had themselves asked for money twice for the same cause. Or perhaps they had sometimes taken what was not theirs—say, something small like a newspaper or even money they had found on the ground—and saw what I was doing as no more serious than what they had done. So they may have recognized an ethical dimension, but decided that it wasn't significant enough to create a fuss.

Politicians seem to specialize in trying to downplay the ethical dimension of their behavior. John Edwards, while married, fathered a child out of wedlock and then tried to get a colleague to take the fall for him. A Massachusetts state senator, too, was arrested in June 2008 for allegedly attempting to grope a woman on the street.[39] He apparently had a record of harassing other women over a period of years. Pleading innocent even after being caught red-handed, he also did something even more dramatically irresponsible and unethical: when asked his name, he gave the name of a colleague in the state senate instead.

4. Take personal responsibility for generating an ethical solution to the problem. The students may have felt that they are, after all, merely students. Is it their responsibility, or even their right, to tell a professor in a course on leadership how to act, especially if the professor is a dean? From their point of view, it was perhaps my responsibility to determine the ethical dimensions of the situation, if any.

Similarly, people may allow leaders to commit wretched acts because they figure it is the leaders' responsibility to determine the ethical dimensions of their actions. Isn't that why they are leaders in the first place? Or people may assume that the leaders, especially if they are religious leaders, are in a uniquely good position to determine what is ethical. If a religious leader encourages someone to become a suicide bomber, that "someone" may feel that being such a bomber must be ethical. Why else would a religious leader suggest it?

5. Figure out what abstract ethical rules might apply to the problem. Perhaps some of the students recognized the problem I created for them as having an ethical dimension. But what ethical rule applies? Have they ever had to figure out reimbursements? Perhaps not. And even if they have, might there be some circumstances in which it is ethical to be dually reimbursed? Maybe the university supplements outside reimbursements, as they sometimes do fellowships. Or maybe the university does not care who else pays, so long as they get original receipts. Or maybe what I meant to say was that I had some expenses paid by the university and others by the sponsoring organization, and I had simply misspoken. Especially in unfamiliar situations, it may not be clear what constitutes ethical behavior.

Most of us have learned, in one way or another, ethical rules that we are supposed to apply to our lives. For example, we are supposed to be honest. But who among us can say that he or she has not lied at some time, perhaps with the excuse that we were protecting someone else's feelings? By making such excuses, however, we insulate ourselves from the effects of our behavior. At first we might be able to argue that not hurting someone else's feelings should take precedence over not lying. Of course, as the lies grow larger, we can continue to use the same excuse. Or politicians may argue that they should provide generous tax cuts to the very wealthy, on the theory that the benefits will "trickle down" to the rest of the population. This way, the excuse goes, one is still treating all people well—it's just that some people are treated better and eventually the effects will reach everyone else.

6. Decide how these abstract ethical rules actually apply to the problem so as to suggest a concrete solution. Perhaps the students had ethical rules available and even accessible to them, but did not see how to apply them. Suppose they had the rule that one should only expect from others what one deserves. Well, what did I deserve? Maybe, in application, they saw me as deserving more because I said I did. Or suppose they had the rule that one should not expect something for nothing. Well, I did something, so perhaps I was only trying to get something back that adequately reflected my work. In the end, then, the students may have had trouble applying these abstract principles to the problem at hand—and then into concrete behavior.

This kind of translation is important. In our work on practical intelligence, we found that there is, at best, a modest correlation between the more academic, abstract aspects of intelligence and its more practical, concrete components.[40] That is, often people have skills that shine brightly in a classroom, but they are unable to translate these skills into action. For example, someone may be able to pass a written drivers' test with flying colors, but not be able to drive. Or someone may be able to get an A in a French class, but not speak French to passers-by in Paris. Or a teacher may get an A in a classroom management course, but be unable to manage a classroom. Translation of abstract skills into concrete ones is difficult, and may leave people knowing a lot of ethical rules that they are nevertheless unable to incorporate into their everyday lives.

If one follows reports in the media, there are any number of instances in which pastors who are highly trained in religion and ethics act in unethical and unscrupulous ways. They may be able to teach classes on ethics, but they fail to translate what they teach into their own behavior. One may tend to be quick to blame them, but as a psychologist, I know that there are also many competent psychologists who are unable to apply what they do in therapy to their own lives. Being a psychologist is no protection against personal strife, any more than being an ethicist is protection against unethical behavior.

7. Prepare for later possible repercussions of having acted in what one considers an ethical manner. One may hesitate to act because of possible repercussions. Perhaps students in my class saw me as grossly unethical, but did not want to risk challenging me openly and thereby potentially lowering their grade. In genocides, opposing the perpetrators may make one a victim. Or one may look foolish acting in an ethical way when others are taking advantage of a situation in a way to foster their personal good. Even before one acts, one may be hesitant because of the aftermath one anticipates, whether real or merely imagined.

We would like to think that the pressure to behave ethically will lead people to resist internal temptations to act poorly. But often, exactly the opposite is the case. In the Enron case, when Sherron Watkins blew the whistle on unethical behavior, she was punished and made to feel like an "outcast."[41] In general, whistleblowers are treated poorly, despite the protections they are supposed to receive.

8. Enact the ethical solution. You sit in a classroom and hear your teacher brag about what you perhaps consider to be unethical behavior. You look around you. No one else is saying anything. As far as you can tell, no one else has even been fazed. Perhaps you are simply out of line. In the Latané and Darley work mentioned earlier, the more bystanders there were, the less likely one was to take action to intervene. Why? Because everyone figured that, if something was really wrong, then someone else witnessing the event would take responsibility. Thus you are better off having a breakdown on a somewhat lonely country road than on a busy highway, because a driver passing by on the country road may feel that he or she is your only hope.

Sometimes, the problem is not that other people seem oblivious to the ethical implications of the situation, but that they actively encourage you to behave in ways you define as unethical. In the Rwandan genocides, Hutus were encouraged to hate Tutsis and to kill them, even if they were within their own families.[42] Those who were not willing to participate in the massacres risked becoming victims themselves.[43] The same applied in Hitler's Germany. Those who tried to save Jews from concentration camps themselves risked going to such camps.[44]

While I write this, the Obama administration fairly recently enacted a health-reform bill. Whether the administration's plan is a good one is obviously debatable, and as a novice in these matters, I cannot offer an opinion. What is interesting, however, is that opposing political figures mentioned the creation of "death panels" that will decide whether a given individual can live or must die. These death panels are total inventions of certain opposition figures that have nothing to do with the legislation. Many of these inventors of this blatant lie are those who speak most loudly about ethics.

Indeed, there seems to be an extremely large gap today between talking about ethics and enacting it. Consider the case of Mark Sanford, governor of Georgia. Sanford was one of the loudest advocates for ethics in government and, due to his marital infidelity and abandonment of his position, may well be one of the least ethical in his own behavior, both inside government and outside of it.[45]

Can Ethical Reasoning and Behavior Be Taught?

Howard Gardner has wrestled with the question of whether there is some kind of existential or even spiritual intelligence that guides people through challenging life dilemmas.[46] Robert Coles is one of many who have argued for a moral intelligence in children as well as adults.[47] Is there some kind of moral or spiritual intelligence that some children have more of than others? Lawrence Kohlberg believed that there are stages of moral reasoning, and that as children grow older, they advance in these stages. Some will advance faster and further than others, creating individual differences in levels of moral development.[48]

The perspective of this book is a bit different. People can certainly differ in their moral reasoning and moral development, but I believe that we can teach children as well as adults to enhance their ethical reasoning and behavior. It is not enough to teach religion or values or ethics. One needs to teach children as well as adults about the steps leading to ethical behavior, as described in this chapter, so that they can recognize in a personal way why and how ethical behavior presents such a challenge. Such an approach will hopefully help them make it through all eight of the steps, despite the many obstacles to behaving ethically.

The Many Barriers to Ethical Action

In the earlier discussion of the challenges of ethical leadership, I wrote of the risk of ethical disengagement.[49] Ethical disengagement is the dissociation of oneself from ethical values.[50] One who is ethically disengaged may believe that ethical values should apply to the actions of others, but not to oneself. One may believe that one is above or beyond ethics, or simply not see its relevance to one's own life.

There are other fallacies that lead people to be foolish. They include

1. *Unrealistic optimism.* The person thinks he or she is so bright, or so powerful, that anything he or she does will turn out all right, regardless of how foolish or unethical it may be.

2. *Egocentrism.* The person comes to believe that his or her leadership or power is for purposes of self-aggrandizement. Tyco CEO Dennis Kozlowski, currently in prison for tax evasion, ran the company as though it were his own personal piggybank.[51] Ethics took the back seat to Kozlowski's desire to enrich himself and his family.

3. *False omniscience.* Some people come to believe that they are all-knowing. The surprising thing about the behavior of a Bill Clinton or a George W. Bush, in quite different domains, is not that they made mistakes, but rather, that they kept making the same mistakes over and over again. Clinton correctly viewed himself as very intelligent, and perhaps thought that his intelligence and excellent education gave him levels of knowledge that he did not have. George W. Bush appears to have believed that he could trust his gut. He was sometimes wrong, but seems to have lacked a higher level of intrapersonal intelligence and self-reflection that would better have enabled him to learn from his mistakes.[52] Barack Obama, during his presidential campaign, made mistakes, but seemed to learn from them and not repeat them. He has since discovered, however, that it is far more difficult to learn from mistakes as president than as a candidate, and as a result his presidency has been marked by controversy.

4. *False omnipotence.* Napoleon's failed invasion of Russia stands as one of the great historical monuments to false feelings of power. Napoleon believed that he was extremely powerful. His invasion of Russia was politically pointless and strategically flawed, but he wanted the prize nevertheless. The invasion was the beginning of the

end for Napoleon. Like so many other powerful leaders, he overreached, and his feelings of omnipotence led to his doom.

5. *False invulnerability.* Perhaps Eliot Spitzer, as governor of New York State, felt himself not only extremely powerful, but invulnerable. As a former prosecutor, he must have known that police agencies had multiple ways of tracking patrons of prostitutes. He nevertheless engaged in a pattern of repeated reckless behavior, which eventually cost him the governorship.[53]

All of the skills outlined here—creative, analytical, practical, and wisdom-based—are essential for success in today's rapidly evolving, global community. The kinds of financial or other investments that may have been "smart" in 2007 are not necessarily smart in 2010, nor will they be in 2020. The social customs that were acceptable in 2000 would seem out of place ten years later. And the material you learn in school can be out of date even before you graduate. The world is changing more rapidly now than perhaps ever before. Someone who cannot cope with novel environments and, most of all, cannot be a lifelong learner, risks failure because the knowledge he or she brings to bear on situations is probably obsolete.

In particular, in life one needs creative abilities to cope with novelty and come up with innovative ideas, and sometimes even to handle familiar situations. One also needs analytical abilities to evaluate whether one's ideas are good ones and practical abilities to execute one's ideas and to persuade other people of their value. Finally, one needs wisdom in order to ensure that one's ideas are ethical, that they will have positive consequences not just in the short term but also down the road, and that they balance the needs of different individuals and groups.

In the context of this broader framework for thinking about intelligence and life skills, current assessment practices for college admissions seem terribly inadequate. Children growing up in challenging environments probably develop high levels of valuable creative and practical skills, because they need such skills to survive—to get to school safely, to study under challenging conditions, and so forth—but these skills are poorly measured by current tests and by high-school GPA.[54] Meanwhile, affluent students enter the school and college sweepstakes with an enormous advantage. In particular, their parents and schools emphasize analytical and memory-based skills, which are easily identified by standard assessment measures, creating a mutually reinforcing, closed system whereby these students are taught what they need to know for standardized tests, score well, and are rewarded with additional opportunities for advancement.

If we are to serve students, colleges, and society well, we will have to break out of this closed system. We will have to insist that more and better tests be used to identify those students who truly have the qualities to lead us creatively, analytically, wisely, and effectively today, tomorrow, and long into this twenty-first century.

CHAPTER 5

ASSESSING HIDDEN TALENTS

If students from diverse socioeconomic backgrounds indeed have substantial hidden talents that are relevant for success in colleges and universities, how can they show these talents to admissions officers?

The problem of documenting a combination of analytical, creative, and practical intelligence has been something of a stumbling block for merit-based alternatives or supplements to affirmative action. My colleagues and I believe, however, that we have derived a system, based on the theory of successful intelligence, that can show such hidden talents not only in students from lower socioeconomic backgrounds, but also in those from higher socioeconomic backgrounds who learn and think in nontraditional ways.

My view that we might have success in this realm dates back at least to a 1996 study in which my collaborators and I gave a test that we had devised to more than three hundred high-school students across the United States. The purpose of the test was to identify students with different patterns of strengths on the basis of analytical, creative, and practical abilities.[1] The study, which is detailed in Chapter 6, showed that when students were taught in a way that matched their patterns of abilities, at least some of the time, they excelled. In other words, the creatively and practically gifted students flourished as long as, at least some of the time, they were taught in ways that matched how they learned. After this study, my colleagues and I went on to show that teaching to all styles of learning does indeed improve achievement relative to teaching in a way that emphasizes just traditional memory-analytical patterns of learning and thinking.[2] But the seeds of a further question were planted in us: is it possible that many students who are not now being identified as having impressive credentials for college or graduate work might in fact be so identified if they were assessed in a way that looked at creative and practical, as well as analytical, kinds of skills? The Rainbow Project sought to answer this question.

THE RAINBOW PROJECT

The Rainbow Project was an attempt to show that one could improve college admissions by using assessments that measure creative and practical, in addition to analytical, skills.[3] The Rainbow measures can supplement the SAT Reasoning Test or the ACT. The SAT Reasoning Test measures reading, mathematical, and writing skills. At the time we did this study, the writing component had not been added. (It is still less used by many college admissions officers, although it is gaining traction.) A wide variety of studies have shown the utility of the SAT as a predictor of college success, especially as measured by GPA.

In the Rainbow Project, data were collected at fifteen schools across the United States, including eight four-year colleges, five community colleges, and two high schools. Participants were 1,013 students predominantly in their first year of college or their final year of high school. In this report, we discuss analyses only for college students because they were the only ones for whom we had college performance data. The final number of participants included in these analyses was 793.

Baseline measures of standardized test scores and high-school GPA were collected to evaluate the predictive validity of current tools used for college admission criteria, and to provide a contrast for our current measures. Students' scores on standardized college entrance exams were obtained from the College Board.

Measuring Analytical Skills

The measure of analytical skills was provided by the SAT as well as by answers to analytical questions on what I have called the Sternberg Triarchic Abilities Test (STAT).[4] The questions are designed to measure the following kinds of skills:

Analytical-verbal: Figuring out meanings of neologisms (artificial words) from natural contexts. Students see a novel word embedded in a paragraph and have to infer its meaning from the context.

Analytical-quantitative: Number series. Students have to identify what number should come next in a series of numbers.

Analytical-figural: Matrices. Students see a figural matrix with the lower right entry missing and are asked to indicate which of the options fits into the missing space.

Measuring Creative Skills

Creative skills were measured by STAT multiple-choice as well as performance-based questions. The multiple-choice questions explore the following skills:

Creative-verbal: Novel analogies. Students are presented with verbal analogies preceded by counterfactual premises (such as "money falls off trees"). They have to solve the analogies as though the counterfactual premises were true.

Creative-quantitative: Novel number operations. Students are presented with rules for novel number operations, for example, "flix," which involves numerical manipulations that differ as a function of whether the first of two operands is greater than, equal to, or less than the second. Participants then have to use the novel number operations to solve presented math problems.

Creative-figural: In each item, participants are first presented with a figural series that involves one or more transformations; they then have to apply the rule of the series to a new figure with a different appearance and complete the new series.

Creative skills also were assessed using open-ended measures, based on earlier work we had done on measuring creativity.[5] One measure required writing two short stories based on one of several unusual titles, such as "The Octopus's Sneakers"; another required orally telling two stories based on choices of picture collages; and the third required captioning any one of a variety of cartoons. Open-ended performance-based answers were rated by trained raters for novelty, quality, and task appropriateness. Multiple judges were used for each task and satisfactory reliability was achieved.

Measuring Practical Skills

Multiple-choice measures of practical skills were obtained from the STAT through these kinds of questions:

Practical-verbal: Everyday reasoning. Students are presented with a set of everyday problems in the life of an adolescent and have to select the option that best solves each problem.

Practical-quantitative: Everyday math. Students are presented with scenarios requiring the use of math in everyday life (such as buying tickets for a ballgame), and have to solve math problems based on the scenarios.

Practical-figural: Route planning. Students are presented with a map of an area (say, an amusement park) and have to answer questions about navigating effectively through that area.

Practical skills also were assessed using three situational-judgment inventories: the Everyday Situational Judgment Inventory (which is movie based), the Common Sense Questionnaire, and the College Life Questionnaire, each of which explores different types of tacit knowledge.[6] The movies present everyday situations that confront college students, such as asking for a letter of recommendation from a professor who shows, through nonverbal cues, that he does not recognize you very well. One then has to rate various options for how well they would work in each situation. The Common Sense Questionnaire provided everyday business problems, such as being assigned to work with a coworker whom one cannot stand, and the College Life Questionnaire provided everyday college situations for which a solution was required.

Unlike the creativity performance tasks, in the practical performance tasks the participants were not given a choice of situations to rate. For each task, participants were told that there was no "right" answer, and that the options described in each situation represented variations on how different people approach different situations.

All materials were administered either in paper-and-pencil format (325 college students completed the questions on paper) or on the computer via the internet (468 college students worked online). Participants were either tested individually or in small groups. During the oral stories section, participants who were tested in the group situation either wore headphones or were directed into a separate room so as not to disturb the other participants.

There were two discrete sessions, conducted one directly after the other, for each participant. The first session included the informed-consent procedure, demographics information, the movies, the STAT batteries, and the cartoons, followed by a brief debriefing period. The second session included obtaining consent again, followed by the rest of the demographics and "additional measures" described earlier: the Common Sense or College Life Test (depending on the condition), and the Written or Oral Stories (depending on the condition). Because of the large number of tests, not all students received all tests, and hence were assigned to different "conditions" as a function of the tests they received. The second session ended with the final debriefing. The order was the same for all participants. No strict time limits were set for completing the tests, although the instructors were given rough guidelines of about seventy minutes per session. The time taken to complete the battery of tests ranged from two to four hours.

As a result of the lengthy nature of the complete battery of assessments, participants were administered parts of the battery using an intentionally incomplete overlapping design.[7] The participants were randomly assigned to the test sections they were to complete.

The analysis described next is a conservative one that does not correct for differences in the selectivity of the colleges at which the study took place. In a study across so many colleges differing in selectivity, validity coefficients will seem to be lower than is typical, because an A at a less selective college counts the same as an A at a more selective college. When we corrected for college selectivity, the results in fact became stronger. But correcting for selectivity has its own problems (for example, on what basis does one evaluate selectivity?), so we opted to use uncorrected data in this report.

When examining college students alone, the sample shows a slightly higher mean level of SAT than that found in colleges across the country. Our sample means on the SATs were, for two-year college students, 491 verbal and 509 math, and for four-year college students, 555 verbal and 575 math. These means, although slightly higher than typical, are within the range of average college students.

There is always a potential concern when considering students from a select sample of universities, especially when the mean scores on the SAT run a bit high. But our sample was taken from colleges with a wide range of selectivity, from community colleges to highly selective four-year institutions. And the standard deviation of the SAT scores for our group was comparable to—if anything, a bit greater than—that for the population at large (at least those who take the SAT). So such a concern would not seem warranted in this case.

What are the basic abilities underlying performance on the Rainbow Assessments? We used a statistical technique called "factor analysis" to address this question. The technique identifies the basic sources of individual differences, called "factors," that underlie scores on a series of tests or other measures. Three meaningful factors were extracted. One factor represented practical performance tests. A second factor represented the creative performance tests. And a third factor represented the multiple-choice tests (which include analytical, creative, and practical). This last result was not what we expected. We had expected instead an analytical factor. The result shows the importance of not only what a test purports to measure, but also of how the test measures it. In this case, method of measurement proved to be very important. That is, when you use multiple-choice tests, what you get are scores that largely reflect not what the tests were supposed to measure, but how they were supposed to measure it, in our case, students' skill in taking multiple-choice tests. Tests such as the SAT and ACT are largely or even exclusively multiple choice, so one can expect similar results.

In this particular study, we wanted to know how much the Rainbow assessments improved prediction of first-year grades above and beyond the SAT. The answer was that the Rainbow assessments doubled prediction of college success over SAT scores alone. If SATs were combined with high-school GPA, the Rainbow assessments still increased prediction by 50 percent. In other words, the new assessments provided very substantial gains over traditional measures.

For those who are interested in quantitative data, let me be more specific. The SAT and ACT are based on a conventional psychometric notion of cognitive skills and have had substantial success in predicting college performance. But perhaps the time has come to move beyond conventional theories of cognitive skills. Based on statistical analyses (called multiple regression), our measures alone nearly doubled the predictive power of college GPA when compared to the SAT alone. Additionally, the new measures predict an additional 8.5 percent of the variance in college GPA beyond the initial 14.1 percent contributed by the SAT and high-school GPA. These findings, combined with encouraging results regarding the reduction of between-ethnicity differences, make a compelling case for doing more to identify a student's analytic, creative, and practical skills as part of the college admissions process. There is evidence to indicate that measures of such a wide range of skills not only have good incremental predictive power, but also increase equity. As teaching improves and college teachers begin emphasizing further the creative and practical skills needed for success in school and life, the test may well become even more predictive of which students will flourish in college and beyond.

Cosmetic changes in testing over the last century have made relatively little difference to the construct validity of assessment procedures (that is, our ability to measure what we want to measure: future success in college and life). The theory of successful intelligence could provide a new opportunity to increase construct validity at the same time that it might reduce differences in test performance between groups. It may indeed be possible to accomplish the goals of affirmative action through tests such as the Rainbow assessments, either as supplements to traditional affirmative-action programs or as substitutes for them.

The assessments described here do not measure all of the skills required for success in everyday life. For example, although I assess teamwork in courses I teach, the assessments I have described do not measure this skill, at least not directly. Moreover, the assessments have not been scaled up to be used on a statewide or national basis. Doing so would no doubt present new challenges, some of which have yet to be anticipated. Moreover, expanded assessments cost more time and money. But when we consider the benefits of opening up possibilities and hope to students of either gender or any ethnic background who learn and think in a variety of different ways, the costs actually may be relatively small. Our society needs citizens and leaders who are creative, practical, and especially, wise, not just those who are good memorizers and are analytically adept. One way to find and develop such citizens and leaders is to emphasize in college admissions the importance of the broad range of skills that leads to an informed and educated citizenry.

The principles behind the Rainbow Project apply at other levels of admissions as well. For example, my collaborators and I have shown that the same principles can be applied in admissions to business schools, also with the result of increasing prediction and decreasing ethnic- (as well as gender-) group differences.[8] My collaborators and I also have found that including creative and practical items in augmented psychology and statistics Advanced Placement (AP) examinations can reduce ethnic-group differences on the tests.[9] And the same principles are being employed in a test for identifying gifted students in elementary school that has been developed by Elena Grigorenko and her colleagues.[10]

Group Differences

Although one important goal of our study was to predict success in college, another important goal, hinted at earlier, involved developing measures whose results are less distinguishable by the student's racial and ethnic group identity. If measures can be designed that reduce ethnic and racial group differences on standardized tests, particularly for historically disadvantaged groups like black and Latino students, they might help level the playing field for college admissions. How did the Rainbow assessments measure up? In short, they reduced overall race and ethnicity differences relative to traditional assessments of abilities like the SAT. The gap seemed to narrow most for Latino students, with black students, too, scoring nearer to the mean achieved by white students for most of the Rainbow assessments, although a sub-

stantial difference persisted for measures of practical performance. Native American students also scored closer to whites
with the Rainbow assessments; indeed, their median was higher
for the oral creative tests, although our very small sample size
means that any conclusions about Native American performance
should be made tentatively. The bottom line is that the Rainbow
assessments decreased ethnic-group differences relative to conventional tests such as the SAT, even as they improved the prediction of future academic success—the very goal of traditional tests
like the SAT and ACT. This result is a difficult one to obtain,
based on past studies, and we believe we achieved it by greatly
expanding the range of skills typically assessed.

THE KALEIDOSCOPE PROJECT

In 2005, I moved from Yale University, where I was IBM Professor of Psychology and Education and the lead collaborator in the
Rainbow Project, to Tufts University, where I became dean of the
School of Arts and Sciences. Tufts University has strongly emphasized the role of active citizenship in education. So it seemed
like an ideal setting to put into practice some of the ideas from
the Rainbow Project. With the support of the dean of the School
of Engineering, Linda Abriola, and the active collaboration,
partnership, and operational leadership of Dean of Admissions
Lee Coffin, we instituted Project Kaleidoscope, an assessment
tool for college admissions that included not only the ideas of
Rainbow, but also a way to find out about a student's wisdom.
Coffin was the chief implementer of this project, and without his
collaboration and the support of the central administration, it
never could have happened.[11]

Goals and Initial Concerns

Kaleidoscope, like Rainbow, was not designed to replace traditional admissions measures such as GPA and the SAT or ACT;
rather, it was designed to augment these measures. The GPA is
typically the single most useful tool in undergraduate admis-

sions, because it provides a proxy measure of so many things. For example, it measures students' academic abilities, especially analytical ones and those related to memory, all of which will be as important in college as they were in high school. It also indirectly measures motivation, that is, whether a student is willing to work hard to achieve success. It further measures conscientiousness and even aspects of practical intelligence, because it indirectly assesses whether students can understand what teachers want from them and then meet those various teachers' expectations. The SAT and ACT, like GPA, provide an assessment of memory and analytical abilities, but they also measure other skills, such as the ability to work under pressure, to make a sustained effort on a fairly long assessment, and to take a multiple-choice test. So our goal was to supplement these and other already existing measures with an assessment that would target creative, practical, and wisdom-based skills, as well as the more traditional analytical ones.

Dean Coffin and his admissions staff placed a new set of wisdom-intelligence-creativity-synthesized (WICS) questions on the 2006–2010 applications for all of the more than fifteen thousand students applying to the schools of arts, sciences, and engineering at Tufts each year. Whereas the Rainbow Project involved a separate high-stakes test administered with a proctor, the Kaleidoscope Project was implemented as section of the Tufts-specific part of the Common Application. It just was not practical to administer a separate high-stakes test such as the Rainbow assessment for admission to one university. Moreover, the advantage of Kaleidoscope is that it enabled us to move beyond the high-stakes testing situation in which students must answer complex questions in very short amounts of time under incredible pressure. The section is optional, and students were encouraged to answer just a single question.

As examples, in the first year, a creative question asked students to write stories with titles such as "The End of MTV" or "Confessions of a Middle-School Bully." Another creative question asked students what the world would be like if some historical event had come out differently, for example, if Rosa Parks had given up her seat on the bus. Yet another creative question, a nonverbal one, gave students an opportunity to design a new product or an advertisement for a new product. A practical question queried how students had persuaded friends of an unpopular idea they held. A wisdom question asked students how an intellectual passion they had could be applied toward a common good. The questions we used during the first four years of the project are all shown in the Appendix.

Scoring of Kaleidoscope is holistic, and does not depend solely on the essays. That is, admissions personnel based their analytical, creative, practical, and wisdom-based ratings on the student's entire application. Thus our goal was not merely to add a new assessment and rate it, but rather to provide a broader way of assessing the entire application through the lens of whether the applicant had qualities associated with the capacity for positive leadership.

Asking students to answer only a single question was a judgment call. Any single question would take students quite a while to answer well, and we worried that if we expected them to answer multiple Kaleidoscope questions, droves of high-schoolers would not apply because it would take so much longer to complete the Tufts application than applications from competitor schools. Moreover, the theory of successful intelligence is based on the notion that successfully intelligent students recognize and capitalize on their strengths, as well as identify, correct, or compensate for their weaknesses. The very act of choosing a single Kaleidoscope essay to write thus allowed applicants to show their skill in capitalizing on one of their strengths.

Kaleidoscope was not created to provide a back door to admission for students who are creative but who are marginal students. Nor was it meant to bar students with outstanding academic credentials from admission. In all competitive admissions environments, the hardest cases to decide on are those in the upper middle of the distribution.[12] At Tufts, the nearly sixteen thousand applicants each year are rated academically on a numerical scale. Students with very high ratings, at or near the top of the academic distribution, have outstanding high-school GPAs and SATs or ACTs. Their letters of recommendation indicate exemplary academic achievement. Students with very low ratings, at or near the bottom of the academic distribution, generally have GPAs and SATs that fall well below those in the typical range within our entering classes. If a student is rated very high on the academic scale, the chances of his or her being admitted are usually strong, but not perfect because personal factors play a role as well. Kaleidoscope is not used in a negative way to reject such students (although indirectly, if one student is helped, another is hurt, given that only a fixed number of students can be admitted to the class). Neither is it used to compensate for unsatisfactory academic records. Academic excellence and achievement remain the central elements of Tufts' undergraduate admission process.

Where Kaleidoscope is most useful is for those in the upper middle of the academic distribution. These scores characterize the large number of students who have strong academic records with signs of both strength and some weakness. (Often the problem is not weakness at all, but merely that, despite a given applicant's strengths, other applicants are perceived as even stronger.) Perhaps their GPAs are very high but their SATs are not quite as impressive, or vice versa. Most students who apply have good records, but the competition is fierce. Among these students, Kaleidoscope helps quantify more explicitly and objectively the positive personal qualities that before had been only subjectively evaluated.

Preliminary Results

We now have all the results of our first year of implementation (class of 2011) as well as some for the second year (class of 2012), and they are very promising. It is important to keep in mind while reading about these results that they are correlational—that is, they represent correlations between what happened when we introduced Kaleidoscope and what happened in admissions. Correlation, however, does not necessarily indicate causation. Many other factors may change as well, any of which can be jointly responsible for changes in admissions patterns. For example, at the same time that we introduced Kaleidoscope, we also introduced a new marketing and communications plan in undergraduate admissions, and substantially increased financial-aid resources as well as our recruitment outreach to minority populations. Dean Coffin and his staff introduced an array of changes to the university's recruitment and selection processes, of which Kaleidoscope was only one part, designed explicitly to enhance our admissions profile.

Some stakeholders worried that, after the introduction of Kaleidoscope, the number of applications would go down because completing a Kaleidoscope essay would involve more work by the applicant. But the university's application volume held steady at recent record levels. Moreover, the quality of applicants rose substantially, with notably fewer applications by students in what before had been the bottom third of the pool. We suspect that many of those students, seeing the new application, may have decided not to bother to apply. Meanwhile, many more strong applicants applied who had perhaps been drawn to Tufts by a new view book, a panorama of life at Tufts designed by the admissions office to appeal to strong applicants.

Other stakeholders were concerned that average SATs would go down and perhaps even plummet. Instead, the mean scores for accepted and enrolled students went up. They have gone up every year since Tufts has used Kaleidoscope. A reason may be that the new assessments are not negatively correlated with SATs. Rather, they just are not much correlated at all, one way or another. So adopting these new methods does not result in less qualified applicants being admitted. Rather the applicants who are admitted are more qualified, and in a broader way. Our studies revealed that high-scoring students on Kaleidoscope tend to be more satisfied with their personal life and their interactions with other students than are students who scored low on the Kaleidoscope questions. They are also more socially active and find their extracurricular activities to be more meaningful. Perhaps most rewarding were the positive comments from the many applicants who felt that our application gave them a chance to show themselves for who they are.

In the course of many speaking engagements, I have been impressed by the positive response to Kaleidoscope by applicants and their parents. There seems to be a widespread perception that the college admissions process today does not typically allow applicants to demonstrate their full range of talents and achievements. Kaleidoscope is viewed by applicants as a way of showing a side of themselves that otherwise would not be revealed.

After several years in which the number of applications to Tufts by underrepresented minorities stayed pretty much the same, the very first year of Kaleidoscope, both the numbers of applications and acceptances of underrepresented minorities rose. This was an instance where Kaleidoscope worked well in conjunction with increased recruitment efforts and increased financial-aid resources. The extra recruitment efforts provided more incentive for students of color to apply, Kaleidoscope helped admissions officers identify the most talented students from all backgrounds, and the increased aid created more incentive for accepted students to matriculate at Tufts instead of a competitor. In the end, Tufts both gained in applications of underrepresented minorities and was able to admit roughly 30 percent more African-American students than the year before, and 15 percent more Hispanic Americans.

Our results show that it is possible, through a diverse set of innovations in admissions procedures, to maintain or increase academic quality and simultaneously to increase diversity—and to do so for an entire undergraduate class at a major university, not just for small samples of students at some scattered colleges.

Most important, we sent a message to students, parents, high-school guidance counselors, and others that we believe there is more to a person than the narrow spectrum of skills assessed by standardized tests, and that these broader skills can be assessed in a quantifiable way.

My experience when I worked as a special assistant to the dean of undergraduate admissions at Yale was that GPAs and test scores served to "anchor" the applicant. The first thing one would notice upon reading an application was the combination of grades and test scores. This combination would establish where on an essentially unidimensional continuum the applicant fell. The resulting mindset would continue to guide subsequent, more detailed readings of the application as well. Other factors such as participation in athletics, student government, and charitable work could move the anchor up or down a few notches. But the main bases for evaluation were grades and test scores. By quantifying aspects of leadership beyond academic skills, Kaleidoscope helps establish a broader basis for anchoring. Grades and test scores still matter, but they can more easily be evaluated in a broader context.

Enrolled Students' Academic Performance

One concern we all had at Tufts was how the students who excelled in the Kaleidoscope Project would do academically once they came to Tufts. Our goal in Kaleidoscope was not necessarily to increase academic performance. Rather, it was at least to maintain the high caliber of academic performance Tufts students have shown while simultaneously increasing admission for qualities of leadership and active citizenship. We have analyzed the results for the first year of the class of 2011 at Tufts. There was no significant difference between those with top Kaleidoscope scores and students of comparable academic credentials (that is, SATs and high-school GPA) but with weaker Kaleidoscope scores. Such students most likely would have excelled in some aspect of the application other than Kaleidoscope. But students who were rated for Kaleidoscope also performed better academically in their freshman year than did unrated students, holding constant their high-school GPA and SAT scores. Thus involvement in Kaleidoscope improved prediction of academic success: rated students had higher GPAs than did unrated ones. In other words, Kaleidoscope appears to have been associated with an increase in the caliber of leadership of the applicant pool and of admitted applicants, as well as with increased diversity of the student body.

This increase, however, is an association: again, one cannot draw causal conclusions. At the same time Kaleidoscope was being implemented, other improvements in admissions were being implemented, of which Kaleidoscope was a part. These improvements were designed better to "brand" Tufts as a school that develops future leaders. My guess is that a system like Kaleidoscope can work very well when the admissions philosophy is compatible with selection for positive leadership and active citizenship skills. I suspect it would work only poorly if it were "grafted" onto an admissions philosophy that was more narrow and parochial in its outlook.

The Rainbow Project doubled prediction of freshman-year grade-point averages; Kaleidoscope did not increase prediction at this stunning level, although participation in Kaleidoscope was associated with a significant increase in freshman GPA. There may be several reasons for this difference. First, Rainbow was proctored in a classroom rather than done at home. Second, Rainbow was timed whereas Kaleidoscope was not. Third, the sample group for Rainbow probably included a much wider range of ability levels than did the group of applicants who chose to answer a Kaleidoscope question. We were able to assess the validity of Kaleidoscope only for students admitted to Tufts, who generally have advanced academic skills: their SAT scores average in the low 700s, and very few accepted students have SAT scores below the high 600s. Fourth, Rainbow raters were blind to the identities of those being rated whereas Kaleidoscope raters were not. Finally, Rainbow had an oral-story subtest—which showed the highest incremental correlations with college GPA—whereas Kaleidoscope did not.

We do not know if Kaleidoscope would have increased prediction more if it had been given to students representing a wider range of abilities. But our goal for Kaleidoscope was somewhat different from our goal for Rainbow. At Tufts, prediction of academic performance, a central objective of the Kaleidoscope project, is not an important issue. Very few students flunk out, and those who do almost always do so not because they lack academic skills but rather because they have problems in their personal lives that overwhelm them. Rather, our main goal was to find a way to predict which students would become more involved as active citizens and as student leaders, and not just be good grade-getters. In this domain, Kaleidoscope did provide valuable, predictive information that we did not get elsewhere.

We now have our first results from the class of 2012. The results are again very promising. Whereas in the first year of the project slightly more than half of the applicants completed Kaleidoscope essays, in the second year, about two-thirds did. This was a large increase, and seemed to show greater acceptance of and enthusiasm for writing essays (or doing artwork) that goes beyond the traditional application; or it may have reflected some students' belief that they needed to answer a Kaleidoscope question to maximize their chances of admission.

As in the first year of implementation, Kaleidoscope ratings correlated best with personal ratings and ratings of extracurricular activities by admissions officers and only very weakly with SATs and academic ratings. This means that the project ratings were valid: they correlated only with what they were supposed to correlate with.

There were no significant racial-ethnic differences as a function of Kaleidoscope score, meaning that the test did not yield different results for different groups. Kaleidoscope also worked equally well for all applicants, not just those in a particular group. As hoped for, higher Kaleidoscope ratings were associated with greater chances of admission because they added more context to the students' candidacies, but lower Kaleidoscope ratings were not associated with rejection, independent of other variables. That is, Kaleidoscope was used to help applicants but not to hurt them.

Kaleidoscope scores were also moderately associated with ratings of students' extracurricular and leadership activities in high school but only weakly associated with their high-school GPAs and SAT scores. So these scores provided a somewhat distinctive look at student capabilities.

Projects like Kaleidoscope can be done at the graduate level as well. We designed an admissions test for a large and highly rated business school in the Midwest, which we showed could increase prediction and decrease both gender and ethnic-group differences in admissions.[13]

More on Kaleidoscope Scoring

One might wonder how one can evaluate answers to questions that seem so subjective. The answer is through well-developed scoring rubrics that we have shown can achieve high degree of consensus among raters (called "inter-rater reliability"), and a targeted training program in how to use these rubrics. Admissions officers should be trained by personnel familiar with the principles underlying Kaleidoscope. At Tufts, we used professional personnel from our Center for the Psychology of Abilities, Competencies, and Expertise. When we launched our pilot study, these experts met with the admissions officers and went over sample essays with them. The admissions officers worked in small groups, guided by the experts, to arrive at a consensus score for these samples. After they got a sense of how the scoring is done, the admissions officers went out on their own and scored sample essays, then came back together to compare their results. Where there were disagreements, they talked about them and tried to arrive at a consensus. Finally, they were ready to go out on their own.

Ratings are holistic, so there is no formula for assigning one level of rating or another. Moreover, as mentioned before, essays are scored for Kaleidoscope in conjunction with all aspects of the application. But it is possible to specify, at least in broad strokes, the kinds of criteria that evaluators can use in judging essays.

One can, for example, assess analytical responses on the basis of the extent to which they are analytically sound, balanced, logical, and organized. An analytically sound argument is one that takes a problem, shows a correct understanding of it, and analyzes it in a way that makes sense. A balanced response takes into account competing points of view and weighs them based on their validity. A logical response is internally consistent. And an organized response is one in which the ideas follow in a logical progression.

One can assess creative responses on the basis of how original and compelling they are, as well as how appropriately they accomplish the task at hand. An original response is one that is novel—different from the others. A compelling response is well crafted and adds value to what is known. And a response is appropriate to the extent it fulfills the requirements of a task.

One can assess practical responses on the basis of first, how feasible they are with respect to time, place, and human and material resources, and second, how persuasive they are. A feasible response takes into consideration practical constraints. A persuasive response convinces the reader or listener that a particular strategy is worth pursuing.

One can assess wisdom-based responses on the extent to which they promote a common good by balancing one's own interests with those of others over the long and short terms, through the infusion of positive (prosocial) ethical values. A response promotes a common good if it makes a situation better, on average, for stakeholders affected by that situation. A response balances interests when it takes into account the needs of not only diverse stakeholders, but also the groups to which they belong. A response considers both the long and short terms when it projects the likely outcome of its being implemented over an expanded time horizon. And a response is ethical when it involves values such as honesty, reciprocity, caring, sincerity, and doing good.

In the Kaleidoscope Project, admissions officers are encouraged, though not required, to provide analytical, creative, practical, and wisdom ratings for each student. As mentioned earlier, the ratings are not based only on the essay, but rather on the application as a whole. This is because we do not believe that the essays on the application provide a unique or somehow privileged view of students' analytical, creative, practical, and wisdom-based skills. They may prompt students to reveal their leadership attributes, but they are not necessarily the only mechanism available to identify such qualities. For example, a student might have provided with the application a short story he or she wrote, a musical composition, or a work of art. These portfolio elements would also help contribute to the rating for creativity. Or the student may describe a successful business he or she started or a social network that he or she created—activities that may indicate a high level of practical skill. Or a student may have helped out in a crisis center, or worked to help poor children achieve better lives. Such activities might provide additional evidence of wisdom-based skills. So our goal was to look at the applicant holistically, rating the applicant not just for academic and personal skills, but also for a range of skills that are likely to be useful both in school and in later life.

Financial Considerations
One might wonder about the costs of a system such as Kaleidoscope. Obviously, having admissions officers read additional essays and provide additional ratings takes time and costs money.

And my goal when I arrived and first started suggesting we look at admissions was to avoid using existing funds for the additional costs that Kaleidoscope might impose. I did not want people on campus saying that I "robbed Peter to pay Paul"—that is, that I took money out of a perfectly fine existing program in order to support the new program that I was advocating. So shortly after I arrived at Tufts, a team of development officers and I started fund-raising for the Kaleidoscope Project. We received several new donations including one rather substantial one that allowed us to hire the additional support we needed in the admissions office.

Another issue that faced me as a dean was how to get support for such a program. One issue that confronts any new administrator who comes from the outside is suspicion that his or her new ideas may not fit the existing institutional culture. Constituents rightly do not want projects and programs introduced that may have worked somewhere else, but that have no place in their institution. So I spent a substantial amount of time during my first year as dean talking to people about admissions and how our admissions process might better reflect our values as an institution. We formed a committee with diverse constituencies to consider ways in which we might enhance an already successful admissions operation.

Tufts describes itself as creating "new leaders for a changing world," and as an institution, it is serious about this goal. The words are not hollow, but rather capture the spirit of a school where relatively large numbers of students genuinely care about making the world a better place. Kaleidoscope seemed to me to be one of many initiatives that would help the college achieve its own aspirations for leadership development. It says more about the university than about me that the reception was almost uniformly enthusiastic. Stakeholders in the university saw Kaleidoscope as one of many projects that truly could help Tufts administrators meet their own aspirations. In particular, Kaleidoscope was embraced by the dean and staff of the admissions office, who viewed the project as one of many means for accomplishing their goals—namely, to admit the best possible students to Tufts.

An obvious question with a project like Kaleidoscope is fakability. The main way to fake on this assessment is to have someone else write it. Because Kaleidoscope, unlike Rainbow, is a "take-home" test (because it is part of the application to Tufts), in theory someone else could write the essay and the applicant could submit it as his or her own, just as with any application essay. Probably there are cases where indeed someone else writes the essays for the applicant, or at least coaches the applicant heavily. But there are features of Kaleidoscope that work against such a possibility.

For instance, unlike the essays in the Common Application, the Kaleidoscope essays used in the Tufts application are unique to Tufts and most of them are different year to year. Hence there is little incentive for a business to start writing Kaleidoscope essays, at least in the same way there would be for Common Application essays, which have a huge market.

It is also not clear that the most obvious suspects for writing the essays, parents or college counselors, would be in any better position to write the essays than would be the applicants. For example, parents might be less able to write a short story on a topic such as "The End of MTV" than would be their children. Parents, in general, would have no more experience with the types of essays we used than would their children, and likely would have less.

In addition, those who might be most desperate for Kaleidoscope to help them gain admittance—those with poor academic records—tend not to be admitted anyway, regardless of their performance on Kaleidoscope. As noted earlier, Tufts needs to ensure that admitted students are academically qualified; if they are not, they simply are not admitted.

Finally, in our experience, many students find the Kaleidoscope essays the most intriguing part of the application and would not want someone other than themselves to do such an essay, because it is a way for them to express their individuality.

ASSESSING ACHIEVEMENT

As noted earlier, we have applied the fundamental ideas of Rainbow and Kaleidoscope to other kinds of assessments as well. In a related project, funded by the Educational Testing Service and the College Board, we asked whether the same principles could be applied to high-stakes achievement testing used for college admissions and placement.[14] We modified Advanced Placement tests in psychology and statistics to assess not only analytical skills, but creative and practical skills as well. Here is an example from a modified AP psychology exam:

> A variety of explanations have been proposed to account for why people sleep.
>
> (a) Describe the Restorative Theory of sleep *(memory-based)*.
> (b) An alternative theory is an evolutionary theory of sleep, sometimes referred to as the "Preservation and Protection" theory. Describe this theory and compare and contrast it with the Restorative Theory. State what you see as the two strong points and two weak points of this theory compared to the Restorative Theory *(analytical)*.
> (c) How might you design an experiment to test the Restorative Theory of sleep? Briefly describe the experiment, including the participants, materials, procedures, and design *(creative)*.
> (d) A friend informs you that she is having trouble sleeping. Based on your knowledge of sleep, what kinds of helpful (and health-promoting) suggestions might you give her to help her fall asleep at night *(practical)?*

We found that by asking such questions, as in the other studies, we were able both to increase the range of skills we tested and substantially to reduce ethnic-group differences in test scores. Thus it is possible to reduce group differences for scores on not only aptitude tests, but also achievement tests.

In sum, the principles of Rainbow and Kaleidoscope can be applied to a variety of kinds of assessment, and at a broad range of age levels. Our hope is that these principles will usher in a new era of assessment whereby applicants will be viewed broadly and holistically, rather than narrowly and in terms of the small bits measured by the conventional tests currently used in admissions.

CHAPTER 6

ENCOURAGING CREATIVITY,
PRACTICAL INTELLIGENCE,
AND WISDOM

It is not enough to consider a broader spectrum of skills and attributes in college admissions. Once a college or university admits students with a wider range of abilities, it needs to teach in ways that reflect how students learn.[1] If a university broadens its admissions policy to value attributes such as creativity and leadership, but then teaches students primarily in a way that rewards how well they memorize, then it is setting up itself and its students for failure.

INSTRUCTION AND ADMISSIONS: A FALSE DICHOTOMY

Instruction is typically seen as an issue separate from admissions. For one thing, faculty members are actively involved in designing their own instruction, but typically are less involved or not involved at all in admissions. Moreover, in colleges and universities, the dean in charge of instruction typically will be different from the dean responsible for admissions. Administratively, this arrangement may make sense. But conceptually, admissions and instruction ought to be closely linked. Once you decide whom you want to admit, you have to decide what kind of instruction they will need. This is true regardless of whether one uses the system I have described in this book. In that system, you would want to teach in a way that appeals to creative and practical as well as analytical learners because you are admitting all such learners to college. But even in more conventional systems, admissions and instruction are linked. If you admit athletes with academic records that fall below the college's typical academic profile, you will need to offer instructional interventions that will help these students negotiate the rigors of college instruction. If you admit students whose primary goal is to excel in music, you will have to provide advanced music instruction that will allow these students to thrive. In sum, methods of admissions and methods of instruction need to be considered together rather than apart.

As a freshman in college, I was determined to major in psychology and to be a psychologist. I took an introductory psychology course that was taught in much the same way many such courses are taught today. To get an A in the course, one needed merely to memorize the lectures and the textbook.

The professor was no softie. He handed back the papers the day before Thanksgiving vacation. He also handed them back in descending order. The idea was that one would get back one's paper, stand up to be recognized, and then walk out of the classroom to enjoy one's vacation. First he handed back the 10s, then the 9s, then the 8s, then the 7s. By the time he reached the 7s, I figured that my paper must have gotten out of order. It just did not seem possible that I had gotten below a 7. The professor continued handing out papers, and worked his way down from 7 to 6 to 5 to 4 to 3. I received a score of 3 out of 10 on that first class test. When the professor handed me back my booklet, he commented, "There is a famous Sternberg in psychology [Saul Sternberg], and it looks like there won't be another one." I was not much of a memorizer, and my grade showed it. I ultimately got a C in the course, which my professor referred to as a "gift."

Discouraged, I decided instead to study mathematics, because it seemed like a practical and potentially interesting major. I took the introductory real-analysis course for math majors and failed the midterm. The professor suggested that anyone who had failed the midterm drop the course. I did. I then decided to return to psychology, believing a C to be substantially better than an F. Despite the weak start, I eventually graduated summa cum laude, with "honors with highest distinction" in psychology. Thirty years later, I was elected president of the American Psychological Association. I was not the only president of the association to have received a C in the introductory course. My predecessor, Phil Zimbardo, now professor emeritus at Stanford, also received a C. He nevertheless went on to become one of the most famous psychologists in the world, known especially for the "Stanford prison experiment," in which he showed how a simulated prison environment could turn ordinary college students into people who thought and acted like sadistic prison guards or dehumanized prisoners.

The kind of experience I had in introductory psychology is by no means unique to that course, or to psychology. Many low-level courses, in college as well as graduate school, are taught in such a way that the goal seems to be nothing more than memorization of facts and concepts. In some schools, especially those with large classes, virtually all tests are multiple choice. What is the problem?

When I was taking third-year French, my French teacher commented to me that it was obvious from the kinds of mistakes I made that I did not have much foreign-language learning ability—that I was succeeding by virtue of general intellectual abilities. She thought that whatever abilities I had for learning English did not extend to learning a new language. As a result of her comment, I never took another course in any foreign language. Knowing that I lacked the ability to learn such languages, I saw no sense in even trying. Better to spend my time, I reasoned, on subjects for which I had an aptitude.

Years later, I needed to learn Spanish for a project I was doing in Venezuela. The project, contracted by the then Ministry for the Development of Intelligence, which was headed by the visionary Luis Alberto Machado, was intended to help Venezuelan college students increase their intellectual skills. And the program that came out of it did just that.[2] Because the program would be taught in Spanish to Spanish-speaking students, I thought I had better learn some Spanish. I was in my twenties at the time, well past the age most people feel comfortable learning a new language. I studied with a tutor and did well. In fact, one day my tutor commented that he could tell from my work that I had a real aptitude for learning foreign languages. His comment was opposite to that of my French teacher.

French and Spanish are obviously very similar Romance languages, so whatever the cause of their opposite comments, it was not that the languages require radically different skills. Instead, the source was the difference in the way they were taught— one by a mimic-and-memorize method, which did not match my abilities well, and the other by a learning-from-context method, which because of my skills I was able to profit from more readily. Indeed, research confirms that one's ability to learn can be affected by the way material is taught. But teachers often teach in only one way—most often by emphasizing memorization and rote learning—so that only students who are good memorizers are able to excel. And because little in later life depends on memorization skills, one ends up with an educational system that is bizarrely inadequate for preparing students for later achievement. One does not have to be a walking encyclopedia to succeed.

FOSTERING SUCCESSFUL INTELLIGENCE

Can we teach skills related to successful intelligence—the kind of intelligence that really matters in life and in jobs? The answer is a resounding yes—research shows that we can not only test for successful intelligence, but also teach in ways that enhance it.[3]

The Relationship between Aptitude and Instruction

A test of analytical, creative, and practical intelligence was administered to 326 high-school students around the United States and in some other countries.[4] Students were selected for a summer program in college-level psychology if they fell into one of five ability groupings: high analytical, high creative, high practical, high balanced (high in all three abilities), or low balanced (low in all three abilities). Students who came to Yale, where the study was conducted, were then divided into four instructional groups.

Students in all four instructional groups used the same introductory psychology textbook and listened to the same psychology lectures. What differed among them was the type of afternoon discussion section to which they were assigned. They were assigned to an instructional condition that emphasized either memory-based, analytical, creative, or practical instruction. For example, in the discussion section that emphasized a memory-based teaching and learning style, students might be asked to describe the main tenets of a major theory of depression. In the discussion group focusing on the analytical approach, students might be asked to compare and contrast two theories of depression. The "creative" group might be asked to formulate their own theory of depression. And in the section that spoke to students' practical skills, they might be asked how they could use what they had learned about depression to help a friend who was depressed.

Students in all four instructional conditions were evaluated in terms of their performance on homework, a midterm exam, a final exam, and an independent project. Each type of work was evaluated for its quality in all skill areas: memory, analytical, creative, and practical. Thus all students were evaluated in exactly the same way.

What happened? First, the investigators observed when the students arrived at Yale that the students in the high creative and high practical groups were much more diverse in terms of racial, ethnic, socioeconomic, and educational backgrounds than were the students in the high-analytical group, suggesting that correlations of measured intelligence with status variables such as these may be reduced by using a broader conception of intelligence.

This result confirmed our findings that different populations can have different intellectual strengths, all as valid as those identified by traditional analytical assessments. Just by expanding the range of abilities measured, the investigators discovered intellectual strengths that might not have been apparent through a conventional test.

We know that these different intellectual strengths are all relevant to schooling because the investigators found that all three ability tests—analytical, creative, and practical—significantly predicted course performance. When complex statistical analysis was used, at least two of these ability measures contributed significantly to the prediction of each of the measures of achievement. Perhaps as a reflection of the difficulty of deemphasizing the analytical way of teaching, one of the significant predictors was always the analytical score. (In a replication of our study with low-income African-American students from New York, however, Deborah Coates of the City University of New York found a different pattern of results. Her data indicated that the practical tests were better predictors of course performance than were the analytical measures, suggesting that what ability test predicts what criterion depends on student population as well as mode of teaching.)

Most important, however, the researchers found that students who were placed in instructional conditions that better matched their pattern of abilities outperformed students who were mismatched. In other words, when students are taught at least some of the time in a way that fits how they think, they do better in school. Students with creative and practical abilities, who are almost never taught or assessed in a way that matches their pattern of abilities, may be at a disadvantage in course after course, year after year.

Improving Instruction in Social Studies and Science

A follow-up study examined how third-graders and eighth-graders learn social studies and science.[5] The 225 third-graders were from a very low-income neighborhood in Raleigh, North Carolina. The 142 eighth-graders were largely middle- to upper-middle-class students in Baltimore, Maryland, and Fresno, California. In this study, students were assigned to one of three instructional conditions. In the first condition, they were taught the course that basically they would have learned had there been no intervention. The emphasis in the course was memorization. In a second condition, students were taught in a way that emphasized critical (analytical) thinking. In the third condition, they were taught in a way that emphasized analytical, creative, and practical thinking. All students' performance was assessed for memory-based learning (through multiple-choice assessments) as well as for analytical, creative, and practical learning (through performance assessments).

As expected, students in the successful-intelligence (analytical, creative, practical) condition outperformed the other students on the performance-based tests. One could argue that this result merely reflected the way they were taught. Nevertheless, the result suggested that teaching for these kinds of thinking succeeded. More important, students in the successful-intelligence condition outperformed the other students even on the multiple-choice memory tests. In other words, to the extent that one's goal is to maximize how much information students can memorize, teaching for successful intelligence is still a superior method. It enables students to capitalize on their strengths and to correct or compensate for their weaknesses, and it allows students to encode material in a variety of interesting ways.

Enhancing Reading Instruction

Elena Grigorenko and her colleagues extended these results to reading curricula at the middle-school and high-school levels.[6] In a study of 871 middle-school students and 432 high-school students, researchers taught reading either analytically, creatively, and practically (triarchically) or through the regular curriculum.

At the middle-school level, reading was taught explicitly. At the high-school level, reading was infused into instruction in mathematics, physical sciences, social sciences, English, history, foreign languages, and the arts. In all settings, students who were taught for memory-based, analytical, creative, and practical thinking substantially outperformed students who were taught in standard ways.

The results of these three sets of studies suggest that the theory of successful intelligence is valid overall. Moreover, the results may indicate that, when put into practice, the theory can make a difference not only in laboratory tests, but also in school classrooms and even the everyday life of adults.

Nurturing Leadership Skills

I myself used insights from the theory of successful intelligence when teaching a course on leadership in the Psychology Department at Tufts University. The course was open to undergraduates at all levels in all fields of specialization, and had no prerequisites. It especially pointed out the challenges of ethical thinking in leadership.[7] Readings for the course came from not only a textbook on theories and research on leadership, but also a book of case studies and two books by leadership theorists who present their own views.

Most important, however, were two additional features of the course. First, in every class except the first and the last, a leader came and spoke to students for about fifteen minutes on his or her leadership experiences. The leaders came from all domains of life, including politics, finance, management, the arts, sports, and religion. The presentation was followed by a question-and-answer and discussion session with the leader that lasted forty-five minutes. Students' interactions with the leaders gave them a chance to develop as well as challenge their own beliefs about leadership.

Second, every class except the last involved an active-leadership exercise. For example, in the first class, unbeknownst to the class, a shill joined the students and pretended to be one of them. After I went through the syllabus, the shill challenged it and complained that it was inadequate in a variety of ways. Students were amazed at the shill's audacity. When he was done with his complaints, I thanked him, then noted to the class that every leader, sooner or later, confronts public challenges to his or her authority. The question is not whether it will or will not happen—it will—but rather, how the leader handles such challenges. Students then divided themselves into three groups and simulated how they would handle public challenges. In another class, students had to "hire a dean." They divided themselves into three groups. One simulated the formation of a vision statement, the second simulated a job interview, and the third simulated a persuasion interview to entice the selected candidate to come. In yet another class, students simulated how they would deal with an incompetent team member, and in another, each of three groups formulated a proposal to improve the university; they then had to persuade the class, the "funders," to fund their project.

Third, I had students do both individual and group projects. The individual projects involved their applying leadership concepts to their own leadership and the leadership of others, whom they interviewed. The group project involved their applying principles from the course to analyzing the leadership of a major known leader. Some of their choices were Bill Clinton, Bill Gates, and Kenneth Lay.

All exams were open book and open note. The idea was to convey to students that leaders are leaders by virtue of their ability to apply what they know to leadership activities. For example, the final exam involved the story of a leader from the time she first took a leadership job until the time she was considering leaving it. The students had to analyze her leadership performance at every step along the way.

TWELVE WAYS TO ENCOURAGE CREATIVITY

It is difficult to change admissions and instruction if, in the end, we are using admissions as a way of assessing conformity to societal notions of the "good applicant," and then we teach in ways that develop the same conforming skills. What chance is there for creativity to develop if colleges praise it but then do not reward it?

Most people can agree that creative ideas are valuable.[8] But they are often rejected because the creative innovator must stand up to vested interests and defy the crowd. The crowd does not maliciously or willfully reject creative notions. Rather, it does not realize, and often does not want to realize, that the proposed idea represents a valid and advanced way of thinking. Society generally perceives opposition to the status quo as annoying, offensive, and reason enough to ignore innovative ideas.

To see this resistance in action, one need only look to early negative reviews of major innovative works of literature and art. Toni Morrison's *Tar Baby* received negative reviews when it was first published, as did Sylvia Plath's *The Bell Jar*. The first exhibition in Munich of the work of Norwegian painter Edvard Munch opened and closed the same day because of the strong negative response from the critics. Some of the greatest scientific papers have been rejected by not just one, but several journals before being published. For example, the late John Garcia, a distinguished biological psychologist, was immediately denounced when he first proposed that a form of learning called classical conditioning could be produced in a single trial.[9]

Creative people are like value investors: they buy low and sell high in the world of ideas. This sounds like an easy, logical thing to do. After all, who does not know that we should buy low and sell high? Yet the evidence suggests that although everyone knows it, almost no one does it. For example, when the housing market was high a few years back, people were buying first homes, second homes, investment homes, and any other real estate they could find. When the market went down, people stopped buying, and at the time I am writing, the inventory of homes is at a record high level. Similarly, when the stock market is high, people often can be found buying on margin and trying to scrape together any money they can find to invest—whereas when the market goes down, people look for alternative investments.

The editors of *Forbes,* a business magazine, at one point decided essentially to put these ideas to a test. They took the *New York Times* stock market page, pinned it to the wall of their office, and threw darts at it at random. They then followed, over a number of years, the success of the stocks in their random portfolio as compared with the success of professionally managed mutual funds. They found that the random portfolio outperformed 80 percent of professionally managed mutual funds. In other words, even highly paid professional money managers do not buy low and sell high.

When I was an adolescent, the trend was to wear extremely tight pants—the tighter the better. I have never liked tight pants, including when I was an adolescent. And that was before we knew that tight pants are bad for a man's health, at least if he wants to contribute to the production of offspring. Predictably, other adolescents snickered at the loose pants I wore. They viewed me as a dork, or something similar. After a while, I found myself beginning to wonder if perhaps they were right about me.

This silly but true story illustrates the main reason it is so hard to be creative: there is both external and internal pressure to conform. When people treat one strangely, one begins to wonder whether one is, indeed, strange. And so one begins to want to change to conform to others, and thereby relieve oneself of the pressure that nonconformity causes.

From the investment view, then, the creative person buys low by presenting a unique idea and then attempting to convince other people of its value. After convincing others that the idea is valuable, which increases the perceived value of the investment, the creative person sells high by leaving the idea to others and moving on to another one. People typically want others to love their ideas, but immediate universal applause for an idea usually indicates that it is not particularly creative. Creativity is as much a decision about and an attitude toward life as it is a matter of ability. Creativity is often obvious in young students, but it may be harder to find in older students and adults because their creative potential has been suppressed by a society that encourages intellectual conformity. Yet anyone can choose a creative approach to life. The following twelve ways to do so are based on the investment framework described earlier.[10]

Redefine Problems

Redefining a problem means taking a problem and turning it on its head. Many times in life individuals have a problem and they just don't see how to solve it. They are stuck in a box. Redefining a problem essentially means extricating oneself from the box. This process is the synthetic part of creative thinking.

A good example of redefining a problem is summed up in the story of an executive at one of the biggest automobile companies in the Detroit area. The executive held a high-level position, and he loved his job and the money he made. But because he despised the person he worked for, he decided to find a new job. He went to a headhunter who assured him that a new job could be easily arranged. After this meeting the executive went home and talked to his wife, who was teaching a unit on redefining problems as part of her course on creative thinking. The executive and his wife realized that he could apply what his wife was teaching to his own problem. He returned to the headhunter and gave the headhunter his boss's name. The headhunter found a new job for the executive's boss, which the boss—having no idea what was going on—happily accepted. The executive then got his boss's job. The executive had used his creativity to redefine a problem.

There are many ways teachers and parents can encourage students to define and redefine problems for themselves, rather than —as is so often the case—doing it for them. Teachers and parents can promote creative performance by encouraging their students to define and redefine their own problems and projects. Adults can encourage creative thinking by having students choose their own topics, subject to an adult's approval, for papers, projects, or presentations; having them choose their own ways of solving problems; and sometimes having them choose again if they discover that their selection or approach was a mistake. (Adult approval ensures that the topic is relevant to the lesson and has a chance of leading to a successful final result.)

Teachers and parents cannot always offer students choices, but giving choices is the only way students learn how to choose. Giving students latitude in making choices helps them to develop taste and good judgment, both of which are essential elements of creativity. In my own exams, I often give students choices in the essays they answer so that they can optimally show what they know.

At some point everyone makes a mistake in choosing a project or in selecting a method to complete it. But teachers and parents should remember that an important part of creativity is the analytic part—learning to recognize a mistake—and give students the opportunity to redefine their choices.

Question and Analyze Assumptions

Everyone has assumptions. Often one does not know he or she has these assumptions because they are widely shared. Creative people question assumptions and eventually lead others to do the same. Questioning assumptions is part of the analytical thinking involved in creativity. In 1966, at the height of a craze in psychology called "behaviorism," it was believed that learning required more than one trial and that the kind of reward one used to build up learning did not matter. John Garcia, a psychologist mentioned earlier, questioned both of these assumptions. His ideas were ridiculed and he had great difficulty getting his work published. Years later, others showed him to be correct and he won the highest honor of the American Psychological Association.

Sometimes it is not until many years later that society realizes the limitations or errors of their assumptions and the value of the creative person's thoughts. The impetus of those who question assumptions allows for cultural, technological, and other forms of advancement.

Teachers can be role models for questioning assumptions by showing students that what they assume they know, they really do not know. Of course, students shouldn't question every assumption. There are times to question and try to reshape the environment, and there are times to adapt to it. Some creative people question so many things so often that others stop taking them seriously. Everyone must learn which assumptions are worth questioning and which battles are worth fighting. Sometimes it's better for individuals to leave the inconsequential assumptions alone so that they have an audience when they find something worth the effort. There is no acid test, but one that people can use is whether they are fighting for something both that they believe in and that they think matters to the world.

Teachers and parents can help students develop this talent by making questioning a part of the daily exchange. It is more important for students to learn what questions to ask—and how to ask them—than to learn the answers. Adults can help students evaluate their questions by discouraging the idea that adults ask questions and students simply answer them. Adults need to avoid perpetuating the belief that their role is to teach students the facts, and instead help students understand that what matters is the students' ability to use facts. This approach can help students learn how to formulate good questions and how to answer questions. For if we always give students the questions, and demand only the answers, we teach them to answer prefabricated questions rather than to ask questions worth asking.

Indeed, society tends to emphasize the answering and not the asking of questions. The good student is perceived as the one who rapidly furnishes the right answers. The expert in a field thus becomes the extension of the expert student—the one who knows and can recite a lot of information. But as John Dewey recognized, how one thinks is often more important than what one thinks. Schools need to teach students how to ask the right questions (questions that are perceptive, thought-provoking, and nuanced) and lessen the emphasis on rote learning.

When I started as dean of the School of Arts and Sciences at Tufts, I was the first dean of that school that Tufts had hired from the outside. Tufts administrators chose an external dean in part because they knew that someone from outside a system is more likely to question assumptions that are deeply rooted among those inside the system. The cost, of course, is that some people become distressed when their assumptions are challenged. These assumptions may be ones on which they have built careers or even lives, and no one wants to risk overturning his or her own apple cart.

Teach Students to Sell Their Creative Ideas

Everyone would like to assume that their wonderful, creative ideas will sell themselves. But they do not. On the contrary, creative ideas are usually viewed with suspicion and distrust. Moreover, those who propose such ideas may be viewed with suspicion and distrust as well. Because people are comfortable with the ways they already think, and because they probably have a vested interest in their existing ways of thinking, it can be extremely difficult to dislodge them from that way of thinking.

Thus students need to learn how to persuade other people of the value of their ideas. This selling is part of the practical aspect of creative thinking. If students do a science project, it is a good idea for them to present it and demonstrate why it makes an important contribution. If they create a piece of artwork, they should be prepared to describe why they think it has value. If they develop a plan for a new form of government, they should explain why it is better than the existing form of government. At times, faculty members may find themselves having to justify their ideas about teaching to the university administration. They should prepare their students for the same kind of experience.

When I was a first-year assistant professor, the second colloquium I was invited to give was at a large testing organization. I was delighted that the company was apparently interested in adopting my ideas about intelligence, even though I was only twenty-five years old. My career seemed to be off to a spectacular start. I took the train to Princeton, New Jersey, and gave the talk I had been invited to give. To my astonishment, the talk was an abject failure. It was clear that most of the audience hated the talk I gave and perhaps me as well. I was greatly chagrined. I went from fantasizing about a dazzling career to wondering whether I would have a career at all.

In retrospect, I wonder what I actually expected. Did I really think that people who were, say, sixty-five were going to come up to me and tell me how they had wasted their lives doing conventional testing and now were delighted that I, at twenty-five, had shown them the light? After all, this is an organization that makes millions of dollars in revenue from conventional tests; it is probably not eager to question the basis for its own revenue. I realized then that selling ideas is hard, and it is harder when people have a vested interest in believing something else. Ideally, people will be open to new ideas, especially those that complement the ideas they already have, but this is not always the case.

Encourage Idea Generation

Creative people demonstrate a "legislative" style of thinking: they like to generate ideas.[11] The environment for generating ideas can be constructively critical, but it must not be harshly or destructively critical. Students need to acknowledge that some ideas are better than others, that is, they have to analyze their ideas as well as generate them. Adults and students should collaborate to identify and encourage any creative aspects of ideas that are presented. When suggested ideas don't seem to have much value, teachers should not just criticize. Rather they should suggest new approaches, preferably ones that incorporate at least some aspects of the ideas that seemed overall not to have much value. Students should be praised for generating ideas, regardless of whether some are silly or unrelated, while being encouraged to identify and develop their best ideas into high-quality projects.

Recognize That Knowledge Is a Double-Edged Sword

Some years ago, I was visiting a very famous psychologist who lives abroad. As part of the tour he had planned for me, he invited me to visit the local zoo. We went past the cages of the primates, who were, at the time, engaged in what euphemistically could be called strange and unnatural sexual behavior. I, of course, averted my eyes. My host, however, did not do the same. After observing the primates for a short time, he began, to my astonishment, analyzing the sexual behavior of the primates in terms of his theory of intelligence. I realized at that time, as I have many times since, how knowledge and expertise can be a double-edged sword.

On the one hand, one cannot be creative without knowledge. Quite simply, one cannot go beyond the existing state of knowledge if one does not know what that state is. Many students have ideas that are creative with respect to themselves, but not with respect to the field because others have had the same ideas before. Those with a greater knowledge base can be creative in ways that those who are still learning about the basics of the field cannot be.

On the other hand, those who have an expert level of knowledge can experience tunnel vision, narrow thinking, and entrenchment. Experts can become so stuck in a way of thinking that they become unable to extricate themselves from it. Such narrowing does not just happen to others. It happens to everyone.

We once did a study comparing novice and expert bridge players. We found that the more expert the bridge players, the harder it was to adapt to changes we introduced into the structure of the game.[12] That is, the experts became entrenched and less flexible in their thinking. No one is immune to entrenchment, including myself. For example, at one point in my career, every theory I proposed seemed to have three parts. (Of course, there were three good reasons for this!) At that point, I was "stuck on threes." Learning must be a lifelong process, not one that terminates when a person achieves some measure of recognition. When a person believes that he or she knows everything there is to know, he or she is unlikely ever again to be creative in a truly meaningful way. An important part of creative thinking, then, is being able to escape from entrenched ideas and thinking patterns.[13]

I tell my own students that the teaching-learning process goes two ways. I have as much to learn from them as they have to learn from me. I have knowledge they do not have, but they have a flexibility I do not have—precisely because they do not know as much as I do. By learning from, as well as teaching, one's students, one opens up channels for creativity that otherwise would remain closed.

Challenge Students to Identify and Surmount Obstacles

Buying low and selling high means defying the crowd. And people who defy the crowd—people who think creatively—almost inevitably encounter resistance. The question is not whether one will encounter obstacles; one will. The question is whether the creative thinker has the fortitude to persevere. I have often wondered why so many people start off their careers doing creative work and then vanish from the radar screen. But I think I know at least one reason: sooner or later, they decide that being creative is not worth the resistance and punishment. The truly creative thinkers pay the short-term price because they recognize that they can make a difference in the long term. But often it is a long while before the value of a creative idea is recognized and appreciated.

One example of having to wait for ideas to be recognized occurred in my own experience. When I was very young, I became interested in intelligence and intelligence testing as a result of poor scores on intelligence tests. As a seventh grader, I decided it would be interesting to do a science project on intelligence testing. I found the Stanford-Binet Intelligence Scales in the adult section of the local library and started giving the test to friends. Unfortunately, one of my friends tattled to his mother, who reported me to the school authorities. The head school psychologist threatened to burn the book that contained the test if I ever brought it to school again. He suggested I find another interest. Had I done so, I never would have done all that I have in the field of intelligence, which has meant a great deal to my life, and, I hope, something to the world. His opinion presented a major obstacle to me, especially as an early adolescent; I was just thirteen years old. But because I surmounted that obstacle, I have been able to do research on intelligence, which has been very fulfilling for me.

Teachers can prepare students for these types of experiences by describing obstacles that they, their friends, and well-known figures in society have faced while trying to be creative; otherwise, students may think that they are the only ones confronted by obstacles. Teachers should include stories about people who weren't supportive, about bad grades for unwelcome ideas, and about frosty receptions to what they may have thought were their best ideas. To help students deal with obstacles and develop a sense of awe about the creative act, teachers can remind them of the many creative people whose ideas were initially shunned. Suggesting that students reduce their concern over what others think is also valuable, although it is often difficult for students to lessen their dependence on the opinions of their peers. When students attempt to surmount an obstacle, they should be praised for the effort, whether or not they were entirely successful. Teachers and parents alike can point out aspects of the students' attack that were successful and why, and suggest other ways to confront similar obstacles. Having the class brainstorm about ways to confront a given obstacle can get them thinking about the many strategies people can use to address problems. Some obstacles are within oneself, such as performance anxiety. Other obstacles are external, such as others' bad opinions of one's actions. Whether internal or external, obstacles must be overcome.

Encourage Sensible Risk-Taking

When creative people defy the crowd by buying low and selling high, they take risks in much the same way as do people who invest. Some such investments simply may not pan out. Moreover, defying the crowd means risking the crowd's wrath. But there are levels of sensibility to keep in mind when defying the crowd. Creative people take sensible risks and produce ideas that others ultimately admire and respect as trend-setting. In taking these risks, creative people sometimes make mistakes and fall flat on their faces. But creative people must be willing to take chances.[14]

I emphasize the importance of sensible risk-taking because I am not talking about risking life and limb for creativity. To help students learn to take sensible risks, adults can encourage them to take some intellectual risks with courses, with activities, and with what they say to adults—to develop a sense of how to assess risks.

Nearly every major discovery or invention entails some risk. When a movie theater was the only place to see a movie, someone created the idea of the home video machine. Skeptics questioned if anyone would want to see videos on a small screen.

Another initially risky idea was the home computer. Many wondered if anyone would have enough use for a home computer to justify the cost. These ideas, now ingrained in our society, were once unproven and considered to be of questionable merit.

I took a risk as an assistant professor when I decided to study intelligence, because the field of intelligence has low prestige within academic psychology. When I was being considered for tenure, it came to my attention that my university was receiving letters that questioned why it would want to give tenure to someone in such a marginal and unprestigious field. I sought advice from a senior professor, Wendell Garner, telling him that perhaps I had made a mistake in labeling my work as being about intelligence. Indeed, I could have done essentially the same work but labeled it as being in the field of "thinking" or "problem solving"—fields with more prestige.

Garner reminded me that I had come to Yale wanting to make a difference in the field of intelligence. And he advised that there was only one thing I could do: exactly what I was doing. If this field meant so much to me, then I needed to pursue it, just as I was doing, even if doing so meant losing my job. I did get tenure at the university, but other risks I have taken have not turned out as well. When taking risks, one must realize that some of them just will not work: that is the cost of doing creative work.

Few students are willing to take risks in school, because they learn that taking risks can be costly. Perfect test scores and papers receive praise and open up future possibilities. Failure to attain a certain academic standard is perceived as deriving from a lack of ability and motivation and may lead to scorn and lessened opportunities. Why risk taking hard courses or saying things that teachers may not like when doing so may lead to low grades or even failure? Even teachers who overtly encourage risk-taking may inadvertently pressure students to "play it safe" when they give assignments without choices and allow only particular answers to questions. Thus teachers must not only encourage sensible risk-taking, but also reward it.

Nurture a Tolerance of Ambiguity

People often like things to be in black and white. People like to think that a country is good or bad (ally or enemy) or that a given idea in education works or does not work. The problem is that there are a lot of grays in creative work. Artists working on new paintings and writers working on new books often report feeling scattered and unsure in their thoughts. They often need to figure out whether they are even on the right track. Scientists often are not sure whether the theory they have developed is exactly correct. These creative thinkers need to tolerate ambiguity and feelings of uncertainty until they get the idea just right.

A creative idea tends to come in bits and pieces and develops over time. But the period when the idea is developing is often uncomfortable. Without time or the ability to tolerate ambiguity, many may jump to a less than optimal solution. When a student has almost the right topic for a paper or almost the right science project, it's tempting for teachers to accept the near miss. To help students become creative, teachers need to encourage them to accept and extend the period in which their ideas do not quite converge. Students need to be taught that uncertainty and discomfort are a part of living a creative life. Ultimately, they will benefit from their tolerance of ambiguity by coming up with better ideas.

Foster Self-Efficacy

Many people often reach a point where they feel as if no one believes in them. I reach this point frequently, feeling that no one values or even appreciates what I am doing. Because creative work often doesn't get a warm reception, it is extremely important that the creative people behind this work believe in the value of what they are doing. This is not to say that individuals should believe that every idea they have is a good one. Rather, individuals need to believe that, ultimately, they have the ability to make a difference.[15]

There is no way to know for sure that an idea is good. There are, however, some questions to ask that will help one find out:

- Is there any empirical evidence to support the idea?
- Does the idea follow from any broader theory whose elements may have support, even if the particular idea is not yet supported?
- Is there some way of testing the idea, even if the idea has not yet been tested?
- Are there similar ideas that have been supported, even if this one has not yet been? and
- Are you willing to pursue the idea in the face of what may be determined opposition? (Because if you are not, you will probably never find out whether the idea would have worked out.)

The main limitation on what students can do is what they think they can do. All students have the capacity to be creators and to experience the joy associated with making something new, but first they must be given a strong base for creativity. Sometimes teachers and parents unintentionally limit what students can do by sending messages that express or imply limits on students' potential accomplishments. Instead, these adults need to help students believe in their own ability to be creative. If students are encouraged to succeed and to believe in their own ability to succeed, they very likely will find the success that otherwise would elude them.

Help Students Find What They Love to Do

Teachers and parents must help students find what excites them to unleash their students' best creative performances. Teachers need to remember that this may not be what really excites them. People who truly excel creatively in a pursuit, whether vocational or avocational, almost always genuinely love what they do. Less creative people often pick a career for the money or prestige and are bored with or loathe their career. Most often, these people do not do work that makes a difference in their field.

Helping students find what they really love to do is often hard and frustrating work. Yet sharing the frustration with them now is better than leaving them to face it alone later. To help students uncover their true interests, teachers can ask them to demonstrate a special talent or ability for the class, and explain that it doesn't matter what they do (within reason), only that they love the activity.

In working with my students, I try to help them find what interests them, whether or not it particularly interests me. Often their enthusiasm is infectious, and I find myself drawn into new areas of pursuit simply because I allow myself to follow my students rather than always expecting them to follow me.

I often meet students who are pursuing a certain career interest not because it is what they want to do, but because it is what their parents or other authority figures expect them to do. I always feel sorry for such students, because I know that although they may do good work in that field, they almost certainly will not do great work. It is hard for people to do great work in a field that simply does not interest them.

Of course, taking this attitude is easier said than done. When my son was young, I was heartened that he wanted to play the piano. I play the piano, and was glad that he wanted to play the piano too. But then he stopped practicing and ultimately quit, and I felt badly. A short time thereafter he informed me that he had decided he wanted to play the trumpet. I reacted very negatively, pointing out to him that he had already quit the piano and probably would quit the trumpet too.

I later found myself wondering why I had been so harsh. How could I have said such a thing? But then I quickly understood it. If someone else's child wanted to play the trumpet, that was fine. But I couldn't imagine any Sternberg child playing the trumpet. It did not fit my ideal image of a Sternberg child. I realized I was being narrow-minded and doing exactly the opposite of what I had told everyone else to do. It's one thing to talk the talk, another to walk the walk. I backpedaled, and my son started playing the trumpet.

Eventually, he did in fact quit the trumpet. Finding the right thing is frustrating work. But my son eventually did find the right thing. Today he is a CEO and already has started two businesses. I never went into business. But businesses and my son are a good fit. He is doing what is right for him, and whether it is right for me doesn't matter.

Teach Students the Importance of Delaying Gratification

Part of being creative means being able to work on a project or task for a long time without immediate or interim rewards. Students must learn that rewards do not always come right away and that there are benefits to delaying gratification.[16] The fact of the matter is that, in the short term, people are often ignored when they do creative work or even punished for doing it.

Many people believe that they should reward students immediately for good performance, and that students should expect rewards. This style of teaching and parenting emphasizes the here and now and often comes at the expense of what is best in the long term.

An important lesson in life—and one that is intimately related to developing the discipline to do creative work—is to learn to wait for rewards. Students often succumb to the temptations of the moment, such as watching television or playing video games, but the greatest rewards are often those that are delayed. In fact, the people who make the most of their abilities are those who wait for a reward and recognize that few serious challenges can be met in a moment. Students do not immediately become expert baseball players, dancers, musicians, or sculptors. And high-school students may not see the benefits of hard work, but the advantages of a solid academic performance will be obvious when they apply to college.

Teachers can help students learn to wait for rewards by offering examples of delayed gratification in their lives and in the lives of creative individuals, and by helping their students apply these examples to their own lives. Teachers should also realize that the short-term focus of many school assignments does little to teach students the value of delaying gratification. Projects are clearly superior for meeting this goal, even if it is difficult for teachers to assign projects as homework if they are not confident of parental involvement and support. By working on a task for many weeks or months, students learn the value of making incremental efforts for long-term gains.

Provide an Environment That Fosters Creativity

There are many ways teachers can provide an environment that fosters creativity.[17] The most powerful way is to be a role model for creative thinking. Students develop creativity not when they are told to, but when they are shown how.

The most memorable teachers are usually not those who crammed the most content into their lectures, but rather those whose thoughts and actions inspired others to follow suit. Most likely, too, they balanced teaching facts and figures with teaching students how to evaluate and explore those facts and figures. For example, I will never forget the teacher who started off my seventh-grade social studies class by asking whether students knew what social studies was. Of course, everyone nodded his or her head. The class then spent three sessions trying to figure out just what it was.

Occasionally I will teach a workshop on developing creativity and someone will ask exactly what he or she should do to develop creativity. Bad start. People cannot be role models for creativity in their students unless they think and teach creatively. Teachers need to think carefully about their values, goals, and ideas about creativity and show them in their actions.

Teachers also can stimulate creativity by helping students to think across subjects and disciplines. The traditional school environment often has separate classrooms and classmates for different subjects and thus may convince students that learning occurs in discrete boxes—the math box, the social studies box, and the science box. Creative ideas and insights, however, often result from integrating material across subject areas.

Teaching students to cross-fertilize draws on their skills, interests, and abilities, regardless of the subject. If students are having trouble understanding math, teachers might ask them to draft test questions related to their special interests. For example, teachers might ask the baseball fan to devise geometry problems based on a game. The context may spur creative ideas because the student finds the topic enjoyable, and it may counteract some of the anxiety caused by geometry. Cross-fertilization can motivate students who aren't interested in subjects taught in an abstract way.

One way teachers can enact cross-fertilization in the classroom is to ask students to identify their best and worst academic areas. Students can then be asked to come up with project ideas in their weak area based on ideas borrowed from one of their strongest areas. For example, teachers can explain to students that they can apply their interest in science to social studies by analyzing the scientific aspects of trends in national politics.

Teachers also need to allow students the time to think creatively. U.S. society is a society in a hurry. People eat fast food, rush from one place to another, and value quickness. Indeed, one way to say someone is smart is to say that the person is quick. The format of our standardized tests also indicates our obsession with time efficiency—many multiple-choice problems squeezed into a brief time slot.

Most creative insights, however, do not happen in a rush. People need time to understand a problem and to mull it over. If students are asked to think creatively, they need time to do it well. If teachers overstuff their tests with questions or give their students more homework than they can complete, they are not allowing them time to think creatively.

Teachers also should instruct and assess for creativity. If teachers give only multiple-choice tests, students quickly learn the type of thinking that teachers value, no matter what they say. If teachers want to encourage creativity, they need to include at least some opportunities for creative thought in assignments and tests. Questions that require factual recall, analytic thinking, practical thinking, and creative thinking should all be asked. For example, students might be asked to learn about a law, analyze the law, and then think about how the law might be improved.

Teachers also need to reward creativity. It is not enough to talk about the value of creativity; creative efforts also should be rewarded. For example, teachers can assign a project and remind students that they are looking for them to demonstrate their knowledge, analytical and writing skills, and creativity. Teachers should let students know that a creative response is one that synthesizes existing ideas with the students' own thoughts, regardless of whether this means agreeing with the teacher's point of view. And when evaluating these responses, teachers need to care only that the ideas are creative from the student's perspective, not necessarily creative with regard to state-of-the-art findings in the field. Students may generate an idea that someone else has already had, but if the idea is original to the student, the student has been creative.

Some teachers complain that they cannot apply as much objectivity to grading creative responses as they can to multiple-choice or short-answer responses. They are correct in that there is some sacrifice of objectivity, and they should let students know that there is no completely objective way to evaluate creativity. But evaluators are remarkably consistent in their assessments of creative work.[18] If the goal of assessment is to instruct students, then it is better to ask for creative work and evaluate it with somewhat less objectivity than to evaluate students exclusively on uncreative work.

Teachers also need to allow mistakes. Buying low and selling high carries a risk. Many ideas are unpopular simply because they are not good. But once in a while, a great thinker comes along—a Freud, a Piaget, a Chomsky, or an Einstein—and shows us a new way to think. These thinkers made contributions because they allowed themselves and their collaborators to take risks and make mistakes.

Many of Freud's and Piaget's ideas turned out to be wrong, too. Freud confused Victorian issues regarding sexuality with universal conflicts and Piaget misjudged the ages at which students could perform certain cognitive feats. Their ideas were great not because they lasted forever, but rather because they became the basis for other ideas. Freud's and Piaget's mistakes allowed others to profit from their ideas.

Although being successful often involves making mistakes along the way, schools are often unforgiving of mistakes. Errors on schoolwork are often marked with a large and pronounced X. When a student responds to a question with an incorrect answer, some teachers pounce on the student for not having read or understood the material, which can cause snickering among classmates. In hundreds of ways and in thousands of instances over the course of a school career, students learn that it is not all right to make mistakes. The result is that they become afraid to risk the independent and sometimes-flawed thinking that leads to creativity.

When students make mistakes, teachers should ask them to analyze and discuss them. Often, mistakes or weak ideas contain the germ of correct answers or good ideas. In Japan, teachers spend entire class periods asking students to analyze the mistakes in their mathematical thinking. For the teacher who wants to make a difference, exploring mistakes can be an opportunity for learning and growing.

Another aspect of teaching students to be creative is teaching them to take responsibility for both successes and failures. Teaching students how to take responsibility means teaching students to understand their own creative process, criticize themselves, and take pride in their best creative work. Unfortunately, many teachers and parents look for—or allow students to look for—an outside enemy responsible for failures.

It sounds trite to say that teachers should teach students to take responsibility for themselves, but sometimes there is a gap between what people know and how they translate thought into action. In practice, people differ widely in the extent to which they take responsibility for the causes and consequences of their actions. Creative people need to take responsibility for themselves and for their ideas.

Teachers also can work to encourage creative collaboration. Creative performance often is viewed as a solitary occupation. We may picture the writer writing alone in a studio, the artist painting in a solitary loft, or the musician practicing endlessly in a small music room. In reality, people often work in groups. Collaboration can spur creativity. Teachers can encourage students to learn by example by collaborating with creative people.

Students also need to learn how to imagine things from other viewpoints. An essential aspect of working with other people and getting the most out of collaborative creative activity is to imagine oneself in other people's shoes. Individuals can broaden their perspective by learning to see the world from different points of view. Teachers and parents should encourage their students to see the importance of understanding, respecting, and responding to other people's viewpoints. This is important, since many bright and potentially creative students never achieve success because they do not develop practical intelligence. They may do well in school and on tests, but they may never learn how to get along with others or to see things and themselves as others see them.

Teachers also need to help students recognize how the fit between a person and his or her environment matters. The way in which a creative idea is received requires an interaction between a person and the environment. The very same product that is rewarded as creative in one time or place may be scorned in another.

In the movie *Dead Poets Society,* a teacher whom the audience might well judge to be creative is viewed as incompetent by the school's administration. Similar experiences occur many times a day in many settings. There is no absolute standard for what constitutes creative work. The same product or idea may be valued or devalued in different environments. The lesson is that individuals need to find a setting in which their creative talents and unique contributions are rewarded, or they need to modify their environment.

I once gave bad advice to a student that illustrates the importance of environment. She had two job offers. One was from an institution that was very prestigious, but not a good fit for the kind of work she valued. The other institution was a bit less prestigious, but was a much better match in terms of her values. I advised her to take the job in the more prestigious institution, telling her that if she did not accept the job there, she would always wonder what would have happened if she had. Bad advice: she went there and never fit in well. Eventually she left, and now she is at an institution that values the kind of work she does. Now I always advise students to go for the best fit.

By building a constant appreciation of the importance of person-environment fit, teachers prepare their students for choosing environments that are conducive to their creative success. Encourage students to examine environments so that they will learn to select and match environments with their skills.

HELPING STUDENTS ACQUIRE WISDOM

The development of wisdom is beneficial because wise judgments can improve not only our conduct, but also our quality of life. Knowledge can and indeed must accompany wisdom. People need knowledge to make judgments—knowledge of human nature, of life circumstances, or of strategies that succeed and those that fail. Yet although knowledge is necessary for wisdom, it is not sufficient for it, because merely having knowledge does not mean that one will use it to make sound or just judgments. Many highly knowledgeable individuals lead lives that are unhappy. Some of them make decisions that are poor or even reprehensible.

Why Teach Students to Think and Act Wisely?

There are several reasons why schools should seriously consider including instruction in wisdom-related skills.[19] First, as noted earlier, knowledge is insufficient for wisdom and certainly does not guarantee satisfaction or happiness. Wisdom seems a better vehicle for the attainment of these goals.

Second, wisdom provides a mindful way to enter deliberative values into important judgments. One cannot be wise and at the same time impulsive or mindless in one's judgments.

Third, wisdom represents an avenue to creating a better, more harmonious world. Dictators such as Adolf Hitler and Joseph Stalin may have been knowledgeable and may even have been good critical thinkers, at least with regard to the maintenance of their own power. But they were certainly not wise.

Fourth and finally, students, who later will become parents and leaders, are always part of a greater community and hence will benefit from learning to judge rightly, soundly, or justly. For if the future is plagued with conflict and turmoil, this instability does not simply reside out there somewhere; it also resides and has its origin in ourselves.

For all these reasons, we should teach students not only to recall facts and to think critically (and even creatively) about the content of the subjects they learn, but to think wisely about them too.

It is impossible to speak of wisdom outside the context of a set of ethical values that lead one to a moral stance, or, in Lawrence Kohlberg's view, stage. The same can be said of all practical intelligence: behavior is viewed as practically intelligent as a function of what is valued in a societal/cultural context. Values mediate how one balances interests and responses, and collectively contribute even to how one defines a common good. The intersection of wisdom with the moral domain can be seen by there being some overlap in the notion of wisdom presented here and the notion of moral reasoning as it applies in the two highest stages of Kohlberg's theory. Wisdom also involves caring for others as well as oneself, along the lines suggested by Carol Gilligan. At the same time, wisdom is broader than moral reasoning. It applies to any human problem involving a balance of intrapersonal, interpersonal, and extrapersonal interests, whether or not moral issues are at stake.[20]

How to Promote Wisdom in the Classroom

There are several procedures a teacher can follow in teaching skills related to wisdom. First, students should read classic works of literature and philosophy (whether Western or otherwise) to learn and reflect on the wisdom of the sages. The rush to dump classic works in favor of modern works would make sense only if the wisdom these modern works had to impart equaled or exceeded that of the classic works.

Students should also be engaged in class discussions, projects, and essays that encourage them to discuss the lessons they have learned from these works, that is, how these lessons can be applied to their own lives and the lives of others. A particular emphasis should be placed on the development of dialogical and dialectical thinking. Dialogical thinking involves understanding significant problems from multiple points of view and understanding how others legitimately could conceive of things in ways different from one's own conception. Dialectical thinking involves understanding that ideas, and the paradigms under which they develop, have evolved, as noted by Georg Hegel.[21]

In addition, students should study not only "truth," as we know it, but values. The idea would not be to force feed a set of values, but to encourage students reflectively to develop their own values. Such instruction would place an increased emphasis on critical, creative, and practical thinking in the service of good ends—ends that benefit not only the individual doing the thinking, but others as well. (Again, all these types of thinking would be valued, not just critical thinking.)

Throughout, students should be encouraged to think about how almost everything they study might be used for better or worse ends, and to realize that the ends to which knowledge are put matter.

It is essential, too, that teachers themselves serve as role models of wisdom. Doing so will probably involve taking a much more Socratic approach to teaching than teachers customarily do. Students often want information spoon-fed to them. They then attempt to memorize this material for exams, only to forget it soon thereafter. In a wisdom-based approach to teaching, students will need to take a more active role in constructing their learning so that their knowledge derives not only from their own point of view (which alone can lead to egocentric rather than balanced understandings), but also from the perspective of others. For example, in history, one might ask whether the term "settler" has a different meaning to those who are settling versus those—such as American Indians in the eighteenth century— who view themselves as already living on the land being settled. In science, one might ask how a new discovery or invention could help or hurt others. In literature, one might ask whether a great literary figure, such as King Lear, was wise, and if not, why not. In a foreign-language class, one might ask whether there is wisdom to be learned from another culture that our culture seems to lack. In mathematics, one might ask how mathematical formulas, such as those forming the bases of building bridges, can create a better life for many people. In art, one might ask how wise versus foolish people are depicted by different artists. And in music, one might ask whether one can appreciate the music of people who have hateful prejudices against certain groups of people (such as Richard Wagner, who despised Jews).

PUTTING IT ALL TOGETHER: A NEW
PHILOSOPHY OF TEACHING

When teachers refer to teaching for "critical thinking," they typically mean teaching for analytical thinking, which involves asking students to analyze, evaluate, and assess what they learn. How does such teaching translate into instructional and assessment activities? Consider various examples across the school curriculum. The first set of sample questions emphasizes analytical skills:

(a) Analyze the development of the character of Heathcliff in *Wuthering Heights*. [*Literature*]
(b) Critique the design of the experiment (just reviewed in class or in a reading) showing that certain plants grew better in dim light than in bright sunlight. [*Biology*]
(c) Judge the artistic merits of Roy Lichtenstein's "comic-book art," discussing its strengths as well as its weaknesses as fine art. [*History of Art*]
(d) Compare and contrast the respective natures of the American Revolution and the French Revolution. [*History*]
(e) Evaluate the validity of a solution to a mathematical problem, and discuss weaknesses in the solution, if there are any. [*Mathematics*]
(f) Assess the strategy used by a winning player in a tennis match you just observed, stating what techniques she used in order to defeat her opponent. [*Physical Education*]

Teaching creatively means encouraging students to imagine, invent, discover, and predict. Teaching for creativity requires teachers not only to support and encourage creativity, but also to be role models for it and to reward it when it is displayed. In other words, teachers need to not only talk the talk, but also walk the walk. Consider some examples of instructional or assessment activities that encourage students to think creatively.

(a) Create an alternative ending to a short story you just read that represents a different way things might have gone for the main characters in the story. [*Literature*]

(b) Invent a dialogue between an American tourist in Paris who needs directions to the Rue Pigalle and a French man he encounters on the street. [*French*]

(c) Discover the fundamental physical principle that underlies all of the following problems, each of which differs from the others in the "surface structure" of the problem but not in its "deep structure." [*Physics*]

(d) Imagine that the government of China keeps evolving over the next twenty years in much the same way it has been evolving. What do you believe the government of China will be like in twenty years? [*Government/Political Science*]

(e) Suppose that you were to design one additional instrument to be played in a symphony orchestra. What might that instrument be like, and why? [*Music*]

(f) Predict changes that are likely to occur in the vocabulary or grammar of spoken Spanish in the border areas of the Rio Grande over the next one hundred years as a result of continuous interactions between Spanish and English speakers. [*Linguistics*]

Teaching practically means encouraging students to adapt and use what they know in real-life situations. Such teaching must relate to the real practical needs of the students, not just to what would be practical for individuals other than the students. Consider some examples:

(a) Apply the formula for computing compound interest to a problem people are likely to face when planning for retirement. [*Economics, Math*]

(b) Use your knowledge of German to greet a new acquaintance in Berlin. [*German*]

(c) Put into practice what you have learned from teamwork in football to making a classroom team project succeed. [*Athletics*]

(d) Implement a business plan you have written in a simulated business environment. [*Business*]

(e) Employ the formula for distance, rate, and time to compute a distance. [*Math*]

(f) Fix a proposed design for a new building so that it will work in the aesthetic context of the surrounding buildings, all of which are at least a hundred years old. [*Architecture*]

Teachers who promote wisdom-based skills will first explore with students the notion that conventional abilities and achievements are not enough for a satisfying life. Many people, even those who appear conventionally successful, feel that their lives lack fulfillment. Fulfillment is not an alternative to success, but rather is an aspect of it that, for most people, goes beyond money, promotions, large houses, and so forth. The teacher will then demonstrate how wisdom is critical for a satisfying life. In the long run, wise decisions benefit people in ways that foolish decisions never do. In this context, the teacher must also teach students the usefulness of interdependence—a rising tide raises all ships; a falling tide can sink them. As students learn to balance their own interests, those of other people, and those of institutions, they will realize that the "means" by which the end is obtained matters, not just the end.

The rewards of teaching all of these life skills are great for both teachers and students, and remarkably, include better performance on the old standby measures used for college admissions: standardized-test scores and high-school GPA. But why should teaching for wisdom, intelligence, and creativity synthesized

(WICS) learning improve a student's performance in this way relative to standard teaching methods? There are at least four reasons. First, such teaching encourages a deeper, more elaborate, and more varied understanding of the material than does traditional teaching, so that students are often able to remember it more readily for a test. It also, because of the variety of formats and methods used, enables students to capitalize on strengths and to correct or compensate for weaknesses when learning something new. And such teaching is more enjoyable and motivational for both teachers and students, so that the teachers are likely to teach more effectively and the students are likely to learn more.

Most important, the hope is that students taught with this more expansive approach, and rewarded with test scores that identify all of these skills, will learn to think wisely, intelligently, and creatively, and to synthesize all of these modes of thinking into positive decisions for themselves and society at large.

CHAPTER 7

IMPLICATIONS FOR STUDENTS, COLLEGES, AND SOCIETY

At the time I am writing this concluding chapter, the United States and much of the world is recovering from a widespread and deep economic recession, probably the worst since the Great Depression. It is a recession that many laypeople and even many experts thought could never happen. For young people, it is their first exposure to economic hard times. They may be stunned that their elders would allow the economies of the world to get into such a mess. A country—Iceland—that had become an international banking center and that once was doing very well was brought to its knees. In the United States, the stock market underwent record declines, and unemployment soared. People cut back even on the necessities of life, and some found themselves without the homes in which they had invested so many of their assets.

There was no lack of finger-pointing. But I believe that some of the blame for the serious economic crisis can be assigned to a source that typically has not been singled out—our educational system, which places so much emphasis on memory and analytical abilities but much less emphasis on creative, practical, and wisdom-based skills.

A central notion of this book has been that successful adaptation to life requires four key skills: analytical or "academic" intelligence, practical intelligence, creativity, and wisdom. Admissions, instruction, and assessment in U.S. colleges and universities, as well as in schools of other countries, primarily emphasize the analytical, academic skills. Tests like the SAT and the ACT, widely used in college admissions, measure one's ability to reason, presupposing whatever everyone thinks or knows to be true. They do not assess creative thinking, where one needs to examine and often to go beyond one's presuppositions; practical thinking, where one has to make one's abstract ideas work under a broad variety of circumstances; or wisdom, which requires one to apply one's skills and ethical sense toward the attainment of a common good.

It is sometimes said that we are where we are because of greed. No doubt greed had a lot to do with it. But one must also step back and ask how we developed a culture where greed was, and to some extent still is, treated with such great respect. One must ask how some of the moguls of Wall Street, educated in the best colleges and at the best business schools the United States has to offer, could have led the whole country, and much of the world, down such a long hole. Why did so few people recognize that the securities bundled from the subprime mortgage market were likely to crash and explode? One could say that the moguls were merely greedy. But there must be more. Wisdom involves recognizing the common good as achieved by actions over the long as well as the short term. Many of those who were making the most money are now without jobs, and certainly being unemployed was not in their intended futures.

The problem is that we have created a closed system whereby we select individuals for analytical (as well as memory-based) skills and then teach in ways that reward these skills but largely bypass other skills, in particular, creative, practical, and wisdom-based ones. This system starts in elementary school and has been fortified by the No Child Left Behind Act, which essentially establishes the dominance of tests of sometimes pedestrian knowledge and cognitive processes. It is not that these facts don't matter. It is certainly important to know how to read. It is also useful to know how to compute the area of a triangle or to know basic facts of history. But this level of knowledge is not sufficient for adapting to a rapidly changing world. If we teach to relatively narrow tests, why would we expect the minds we develop to be able to handle the enormous challenges that await them as adult members of a global community?

In essence, we risk rewarding the wrong people, and then developing the wrong skills in those and other people. We admit people to college on the basis of skills that may well matter somewhat for academic performance, but that later in life will be only a small subset of the skills needed for job success. My view is perhaps self-justifying: I earned only a C in the introductory course in my later field of specialization, psychology. But really—how many of the facts that I did not memorize did I later need in order to be a professor at Yale, a dean at Tufts, or a president of the American Psychological Association? It is important to have a knowledge base, but it is more important, I believe, to learn how to use that knowledge base to make a positive difference to the world, at whatever level.

So this book is about how we should change the way we admit students and then educate them to prepare for the challenges they really will face at work and in their personal lives. It is about going beyond statewide mastery tests, SATs, ACTs, LSATs, and the rest—tests that have become entrenched in our society and that have rewarded people who, although they may be adept analytically, have made a mess of the U.S. and even the world economies. We can do better, and this book suggests one validated way in which we might begin.

I have discovered over the course of a career that moving from the idea to the implementation phase in education research is extremely challenging—when education takes three steps forward, it may later take three steps back, four steps back, or even two steps sideways. The obstacles are obvious. First, there is a great vested interest in the instruments we have now, which have changed very little over the past hundred years. Admissions officers are comfortable with them. Testing companies make money from them. Children of privileged classes tend to do better on them, so for the most part the adults of these classes do not rock the boat (and those adults who are least powerful, whose children are not performing as well, are generally listened to least; they can't rock the boat). In addition, there is voluminous evidence to indicate that conventional standardized tests of cognitive skills predict moderately well success both in college and in later life. Moreover, the assessments I have proposed in this book are not panaceas. They alone are not going to turn the world around because regardless of what assessments we use, there will still be people who see ways of taking advantage of others, who advance their own interests at others' expense.

That said, I do believe, based on evidence in the field, that the augmented theory of successful intelligence provides a way to improve on the system we have. It would help colleges recognize students who have the creative, practical, and wisdom-based abilities to make the college campus, and the world, a better place. My hope is that after seeing the success of the Kaleidoscope Program for Tufts, other colleges will choose to adopt it. The data are new—some are not yet even published—so the jury is still out on whether my hope will be realized.

Several years ago, I was approached by a group of psychologists who wanted me to run for president of the American Psychological Association. My first reaction was not to run, because I did not believe I had the leadership qualities needed to head up the association. But I had a mission in mind that I thought was important—unifying what had been a diverse and at times fractious organization. So I made what at the time seemed to me like a strange decision. I would act like a candidate, knowing all along that the whole thing was nothing more than role-playing. This way, I could create campaign buttons and slogans, shake a lot of hands, slap a lot of backs, and act in ways I did not think I had it in me to act. It would be a new personal challenge—and something of a game. Within a few months, however, I forgot that I was playacting, and became psychologically an actual candidate. Once I made the decision to run, the rest neatly fell into place. It seems that we all have the power, in large measure, to decide what roles we want to play in life, who we want to be. But colleges need to empower students so that they too, will believe they can be who they want to be. The concept of successful intelligence provides one means toward such empowerment.

Frank Rich has written an op-ed entitled "The Brightest Are Not Always the Best," a takeoff on the Halberstam book *The Best and the Brightest*.[1] In his article, Rich reminds us how people who are very bright can compromise not only their own position, but their country's as well. For example, Robert McNamara and McGeorge Bundy were prodigies but made a total mess of Vietnam. Bundy's being the youngest dean in Harvard's history did not save him from disaster. More recently, the once-brilliant Donald Rumsfeld helped craft the controversial war in Iraq. An article in the *New York Times* commented on the rise, fall, and rise again of the brilliant economist Lawrence Summers, erstwhile president of Harvard, whose public comments sometimes put him at odds with many of his Harvard constituencies.[2] Bernard Madoff, too, seems to have been brilliant, but used his great intellect to devise the largest Ponzi scheme in financial history.[3]

Some may argue that a great feature of the United States is that there are no uniform criteria for college admissions. If a student cannot get in one place, chances are good he or she can get into another place. The more selective schools have similarities in their admissions processes, but even these schools frequently reach different decisions on the same candidates. Thus almost any student who has done reasonably good work in high school will have multiple options available for attending college. All of this is true. But just because the current system is serving many students well does not mean that little is at stake. Those whose talents and abilities are not well recognized by the current system may well be tomorrow's inventors, community leaders, and generators of fresh ideas in the arts, music, business, and the sciences—if we only learn to recognize their potential and give them the education they need to shine.

This book has suggested that the term "bright" is used too narrowly. People with stellar academic credentials are not necessarily creative, practical, or wise. Such people often capitalize on their strengths, but if they don't manage to come to a full understanding of their weaknesses, and develop ways to correct or compensate for them, they may find that they are their own worst enemies.

A major theme of this book is that abilities are not fixed, but rather, changeable. When I decided that I could act my way into being a candidate, I was deciding that I could transform myself, even if it meant faking it for a while. When students start college, they too often feel like they are faking it—they are uncomfortable in their new role as college students. This discomfort, however, is part and parcel of the undergraduate experience. For the whole purpose of a college education is to transform the individual—to empower students to remold themselves through knowledge, whether that knowledge is acquired in the classroom or during late-night conversations in the dorms.

Life itself is about adapting to new roles. Young people who can think creatively, analytically, practically, and wisely will be ready for not only the formative experience of their years at college, but also the many changes to come in their adult lives, whether on the job or as they build their own families or other communities. Colleges should select students on the basis of how well they have developed these skills, because these are the students who are most likely to succeed after graduation.

For over a hundred years, the way we have admitted students to college has been based on models of human beings that are, at best, incomplete. These models have emphasized, at different points, socioeconomic status, memory-based and analytical abilities, the particular group or groups to which one happens to belong, and other similar factors. I have recommended in this book that the time has come to think more broadly. We should admit students on the basis of merit, but a broader kind of merit that takes into account not only memory and analytical skills, but also creative skills, practical skills, and wisdom-based skills, including ethical ones. Once students are admitted to college, we should then teach and assess their performance using a similar model.

Mine is not the only broad model of abilities. There are many others, such as those of Howard Gardner, Joseph Renzulli, Stephen Ceci, and other psychologists.[4] Ultimately, these models, which seek to improve on earlier models, will themselves be replaced by still better ones. I have suggested here that we use a relatively new model of human abilities, my own, as a basis for admissions, instruction, and assessment. But I would be quite satisfied if any of a number of the broad-based alternatives became widely used. Our children, and the colleges and universities they attend, deserve better than the antiquated, unevenly successful system currently in place. It is time for colleges to use twenty-first-century science to identify, select, and nurture tomorrow's potential leaders for the good of the individuals who apply, the institutions to which they apply, and ultimately, the world.

KALEIDOSCOPE QUESTIONS FOR
THE CLASSES OF 2011–2014

The questions below have been included since 2007 with the Tufts application for undergraduate admissions. Students were invited to select one to answer if they wished. Responses were used to help evaluate the student's analytical, creative, practical, and wisdom-based skills; other data in the application also could factor into these ratings. Questions were used to provide additional information that could only be used for acceptance, not as a reason to reject the applicant. That is, a strong answer could serve as a positive factor in a decision, but a weak answer was not used as a negative factor. Answers were evaluated holistically by admissions officers.

In general, high analytical skills are indicated by responses that are analytical, logical, organized, and balanced. High creative skills are indicated by responses that are novel, compelling, and task appropriate. High practical skills are indicated by responses that are feasible with respect to time, place, and human and material resources, and that are persuasive. And high wisdom-based skills are indicated by responses that show a balancing of intrapersonal (one's own), interpersonal (others'), and extrapersonal (beyond individuals') interests, over the long as well as the short term, through the infusion of positive ethical values, toward a common good.

CLASS OF 2011

Tufts is dedicated to developing leaders who will address the intellectual and social challenges of the new century. Critical thinking, creativity, practicality, and wisdom are four elements of successful leadership, and the following topics offer you an opportunity to illustrate the various elements of your leadership skills. We invite you to choose one of these optional essays and prepare an essay of 250–400 words.

1. The late scholar James O. Freedman referred to libraries as "essential harbors on the voyage toward understanding ourselves." What work of fiction or nonfiction would you include in your personal library? Why?

2. An American adage states that "curiosity killed the cat." If that is correct, why do we celebrate people like Galileo, Lincoln, and Gandhi, individuals who imagined long-standing problems in new ways or who defied conventional thinking to achieve great results?

3. History's great events often turn on small moments. For example, what if Rosa Parks had given up her seat on that bus? What if Pope John Paul I had not died after a month in office in 1978? What if Gore had beaten Bush in Florida and won the 2000 U.S. presidential election? Using your knowledge of American or world history, choose a defining moment and imagine an alternate historical scenario if that key event had played out differently.

4. Create a short story using one of the following topics:
   a. The End of MTV
   b. Confessions of a Middle-School Bully
   c. The Professor Disappeared
   d. The Mysterious Lab

5. Describe a moment in which you took a risk and

achieved an unexpected goal. How did you persuade others to follow your lead? What lessons do you draw from
this experience? You may reflect on examples from your
academic, extracurricular, or athletic experiences.

6. A high-school curriculum does not always afford much
   intellectual freedom. Describe one of your unsatisfied intellectual passions. How might you apply this interest to
   serve the common good and make a difference in society?

7. Using an 8.5 x 11-inch sheet of paper, illustrate an ad for
   a movie, design a house, make an object better, or illustrate an ad for an object of your choice.

CLASS OF 2012

Tufts develops leaders who will address the intellectual and social challenges of the new century, and critical thinking, creativity, practicality, and wisdom are four elements of successful
leadership. The following topics offer you an opportunity to illustrate these various elements. We invite you to choose one and
prepare an essay of 250–400 words.

1. In *The Happy Life,* Charles Eliot called books "the quiet-
   est and most constant of friends . . . the most accessible
   and wisest of counselors, and the most patient of teachers." What work of fiction or nonfiction changed the way
   you live or the way you see the world? Why?

2. Thomas Edison believed invention required "a good
   imagination and a pile of junk." What inspires your original thinking? How might you apply your ingenuity to
   serve the common good and make a difference in society?

3. The human narrative is replete with memorable characters like America's Johnny Appleseed, ancient Greece's
   Perseus, or the Fox Spirits of East Asia. Imagine one of
   humanity's storied figures is alive and working in the
   world today. Why does Eric the Red have a desk job?

Would Shiva be a general or a diplomat? Is Quetzalcoatl trapped in a zoo? In short, connect your chosen figure to the contemporary world and imagine the life he/she/it might lead.

4. Engineers and scientists like astronomer Edwin Powell Hubble discover new solutions to contemporary issues. "Equipped with his five senses," Hubble said, "man explores the universe around him and calls the adventure Science." Using your knowledge of scientific principles, identify "an adventure" in science you would like to study and tell us how you would design an investigation to address it. What solution do you hope to find and why?

5. Create a short story using one of the following topics:
   a. One Way Ticket
   b. "Do Not Push"
   c. Gorillas or Guerillas?
   d. Toast
   e. The Back Seat on the School Bus

6. Every day, people make decisions that force them beyond their comfort levels. Perhaps you moved to a different country or left behind your neighborhood friends to attend a school outside your home district. Maybe you have a political, social, or cultural viewpoint that is not shared by the rest of your school, family, or community. Where did you find the courage to create a better opportunity for yourself or others? How did you find the voice to stand up for something in which you passionately believed? Why did you persevere when the odds were against you?

7. Use an 8.5 x 11-inch sheet of paper to create something. You can blueprint your future home, create a new product, design a costume or a theatrical set, compose a score, or do something entirely different. Let your imagination wander.

8. A high-school curriculum does not always afford much intellectual freedom. As you anticipate your undergraduate experience, describe one of your unsatisfied intellectual passions. Why does this subject intrigue you?

CLASS OF 2013

Tufts develops leaders who will address the intellectual and social challenges of the new century. Since critical thinking, creativity, practicality, and wisdom are four elements of successful leadership, the following topics offer you an opportunity to illustrate these various characteristics. We invite you to choose one and prepare an essay of 250–400 words. (And it really *is* optional!)

1. Since the silent movies of the 1920s first flickered on the screen, the medium of film has inspired, provoked, entertained, and educated. Select a film whose message or imagery resonated with you long after the credits rolled. How did it capture your imagination or affect your consciousness?

2. Engineers and scientists like astronomer Edwin Powell Hubble discover new solutions to contemporary issues. "Equipped with his five senses," Hubble said, "man explores the universe around him and calls the adventure Science." Using your knowledge of scientific principles, identify an "adventure" in science you would like to pursue and tell us how you would investigate it.

3. The 44th president of the United States will be inaugurated on January 20, 2009. If the 2008 presidential primaries were an indicator, young voters will have had a substantial voice in the selection of the next American president. Offer an open letter to the new president: what issue would you like to see addressed in the first 100 days of the new administration? Why does this matter to you?

4. The human narrative is replete with memorable characters like America's Johnny Appleseed, ancient Greece's

Perseus, or the Fox Spirits of East Asia. Imagine one of humanity's storied figures is alive and working in the world today. Why does Joan of Arc have a desk job? Would Shiva be a general or a diplomat? Is Quetzalcoatl trapped in a zoo? In short, connect your chosen figure to the contemporary world and imagine the life he/she/it might lead.

5. People face challenges every day. Some make decisions that force them beyond their comfort levels. Maybe you have a political, social, or cultural viewpoint that is not shared by the rest of your school, family, or community. Did you find the courage to create a better opportunity for yourself or others? Were you able to find the voice to stand up for something you passionately supported? How did you persevere when the odds were against you?

6. Use an 8.5 x 11-inch sheet of paper to create something. You can blueprint your future home, create a new product, draw a cartoon strip, design a costume or a theatrical set, compose a score, or do something entirely different. Let your imagination wander.

7. Use one of the following topics to create a short story:
   a. The Spam Filter
   b. Seventeen Minutes Ago . . .
   c. Two by Two
   d. Facebook
   e. Now There's the Rub . . .
   f. No Whip Half-Caf Latte
   g. The Eleventh Commandment

CLASS OF 2014

Tufts develops leaders who will address the intellectual and social challenges of the new century. Since critical thinking, creativity, practicality, and wisdom are four elements of successful leadership, the following topics offer you an opportunity to illustrate these various characteristics. We invite you to choose one and prepare an essay of 250 to 400 words. (And it really is optional!)

1. It's 1781 and the American colonies have just been defeated by the British at Yorktown. Imagine history without the United States as we know it.
2. Are we alone?
3. French anthropologist Claude Lévi-Strauss observed, "The scientist is not a person who gives the right answers; he's one who asks the right questions." Using your knowledge of scientific and/or mathematical principles, identify a question whose answer you seek and tell us how you might go about investigating it.
4. Kermit the Frog famously lamented, "It's not easy being green." Do you agree?
5. OMG, LOL . . . Texting, cell phones, blogs, and tweets are redefining the way we communicate. Facebook is the new playground while print newspapers are dying. As thumbs replace tongues, does this shift in human expression enhance or limit social interaction and dialogue? Why?
6. a. Use an 8.5 x 11-inch sheet of paper to create something. You can blueprint your future home, create a new product, draw a cartoon strip, design a costume or theatrical set, compose a score, or do something entirely different. Let your imagination wander. OR b. Share a one-minute video that says something about you. Upload it to YouTube or another easily accessible website, and give us the URL.
7. Write a short story using one of the following topics:
   a. House of Cards
   b. The Poor Sport
   c. Drama at the Prom
   d. Election Night 2044
   e. The Getaway

8. People face challenges every day. Some make decisions that force them beyond their comfort levels. Maybe you have a political, social, or cultural viewpoint that is not shared by the rest of your school, family, or community. Did you find the courage to create a better opportunity for yourself or others? Were you able to find the voice to stand up for something you passionately supported? How did you persevere when the odds were against you?

NOTES

1. COLLEGE ADMISSIONS AND TESTING

1. Timeline of the Tyco International Scandal (2005), http://www.usatoday.com/money/industries/manufacturing/2005–06–17-tyco-timeline_x.htm (retrieved June 5, 2008).

2. F. L. Schmidt and J. E. Hunter, "The Validity and Utility of Selection Methods in Personnel Psychology: Practical and Theoretical Implications of Eighty-five Years of Research Findings," *Psychological Bulletin* 124 (1998): 262–274.

3. L. Iacocca, *Where Have All the Leaders Gone?* (New York: Scribner's, 2008).

4. P. Sacks, *Tearing Down the Gates: Confronting the Class Divide in American Education* (Berkeley: University of California Press, 2007).

5. R. K. Merton, "The Matthew Effect in Science," *Science* 159, no. 3810 (1968): 56–63.

6. R. Zwick and J. G. Green, "New Perspectives on the Correlation of SAT Scores, High School Grades, and Socioeconomic Factors," *Journal of Educational Measurement* 44 (2007): 23–45.

7. D. Byrne, *The Attraction Paradigm* (New York: Academic Press, 1971).

8. C. M. Steele and J. Aronson, "Stereotype Threat and the Intellectual Test Performance of African-Americans," *Journal of Personality and Social Psychology* 69 (1995): 797–811.

9. M. C. Frey and D. K. Detterman, "Scholastic Assessment or *g*? The Relationship between the Scholastic Assessment Test and General Cognitive Ability," *Psychological Science* 15 (2004): 373–378.

10. R. J. Sternberg and D. K. Detterman, eds., *What Is Intelligence?*

Contemporary Viewpoints on Its Nature and Definition (Norwood, N.J.: Ablex, 1986).

11. K. W. Arensen, "CUNY Plans to Raise Its Admissions Standards," http://www.nytimes.com/2007/07/28/education/28cuny.html, 2007 (retrieved December 20, 2008). See also "Correspondence between the Florida Multiple Assessment Programs and Services (MAPS) and the Scholastic Aptitude Tests (SAT) at Miami-Dade Community College Based on Students Who Wrote Both Tests," Research Report no. 87–21, http://eric.ed.gov, 1987 (retrieved December 20, 2008).

12. E. Hoover, "SAT Scores Launder Students' Background, Study Finds," http://chronicle.com/daily/2004/06/2004060302n.htm, June 3, 2004 (retrieved December 6, 2008).

13. N. Mackintosh, *IQ and Human Intelligence*, 2d ed. (Oxford, Eng.: Oxford University Press, forthcoming).

14. R. J. Sternberg, *Successful Intelligence* (New York: Plume, 1997).

15. A. Binet and T. Simon, *The Development of Intelligence in Children*, trans. E. S. Kite (Baltimore, Md.: Williams & Wilkins, 1916).

16. R. Herrnstein and C. Murray, *The Bell Curve* (New York: Free Press, 1994).

17. "Metro News Briefs, Connecticut: Judge Rules That Police Can Bar High IQ Scores (1999)," http://query.nytimes.com/gst/fullpage.html?res=9A06E2DB143DF93AA3575AC0A96F958260, 1999 (retrieved December 6, 2008).

18. A. R. Jensen, *The g Factor* (Westport, Conn.: Praeger, 1998). See also essays in R. J. Sternberg and E. L. Grigorenko, eds., *The General Factor of Intelligence: How General Is It?* (Mahwah, N.J.: Lawrence Erlbaum, 2002).

19. C. Spearman, *The Abilities of Man* (New York: Macmillan, 1927).

20. H. Gardner, *Multiple Intelligences: New Horizons in Theory and Practice* (New York: Basic Books, 2006).

21. R. J. Sternberg, C. Powell, P. A. McGrane, and S. McGregor, "Effects of a Parasitic Infection on Cognitive Functioning," *Journal of Experimental Psychology: Applied* 3 (1997): 67–76.

2. HOW WE GOT HERE

1. "Types of Applicants," http://bealonghorn.utexas.edu/freshmen/after-you-apply/applicant-types/index.html, 2008 (retrieved December 21, 2008).

2. See N. Lemann, *The Big Test: The Secret History of the American Meritocracy* (New York: Farrar, Straus & Giroux, 1999); J. Karabel,

The Chosen: The Hidden History of Admission and Exclusion at Harvard, Yale, and Princeton (New York: Mariner, 2006); and D. Golden, *The Price of Admission* (New York: Crown, 2006).

3. See "SAT Reasoning Test," http://www.collegeboard.com/student/testing/sat/about/SATI.html, 2008 (retrieved December 7, 2008).

4. See "The Writing Section," http://www.collegeboard.com/student/testing/sat/about/sat/writing.html, 2008 (retrieved December 7, 2008).

5. See "The Essay," http://www.collegeboard.com/student/testing/sat/prep_one/essay/pracStart.html, 2008 (retrieved December 7, 2008).

6. See "Scoring Guide," http://www.collegeboard.com/student/testing/sat/about/sat/essay_scoring.html, 2008 (retrieved December 7, 2008).

7. See "The ACT," http://www.actstudent.org/, 2008 (retrieved December 7, 2008).

8. L. Okagaki and R. J. Sternberg, "Parental Beliefs and Children's School Performance," *Child Development* 64, no. 1 (1993): 36–56.

9. See "The Common Application," https://www.commonapp.org/CommonApp/default.aspx, 2008 (retrieved December 7, 2008).

10. "2008–2009 First-Year Common Application," https://www.commonapp.org/CommonApp/Docs/downloadforms/CombinedFirstYearForms2009.pdf, 2008 (retrieved December 7, 2008).

11. R. J. Sternberg, "Cost-Benefit Analysis of the Yale Admissions Office Interview," *College and University* 48 (1973): 154–164.

12. J. F. Gubrium and J. A. Holstein, eds., *Handbook of Interview Research: Context and Method* (Thousand Oaks, Calif.: Sage, 2001).

13. "Halo Effect," http://changingminds.org/explanations/theories/halo_effect.htm, 2008; and "Halo Effect," http://www.overcomingbias.com/2007/11/halo-effect.html, 2007 (both retrieved December 20, 2008).

3. ALTERNATIVE ADMISSIONS PRACTICES

1. W. G. Bowen and D. Bok, *The Shape of the River: Long-Term Consequences of Considering Race in College and University Admissions* (Princeton, N.J.: Princeton University Press, 2000); W. G. Bowen, M. A. Kurzweil, and E. M. Tobin, *Equity and Excellence in American Higher Education* (Charlottesville: University of Virginia Press, 2006).

2. T. P. Smith, "Westchester Opinion: Why Not a College Admissions Lottery," *New York Times,* http://query.nytimes.com/gst/fullpage.html?res=950DE6D91F3FF93BA25755C0A96F948260, 2008 (retrieved December 6, 2008).

3. J. Karabel, "The New College Try," http://www.nytimes.com/2007/09/24/opinion/24karabel.html, 2007 (retrieved July 28, 2008).

4. A NEW WAY OF LOOKING AT INTELLIGENCE AND SUCCESS

1. "Intelligence and Its Measurement: A Symposium," *Journal of Educational Psychology* 12 (1921): 123–147, 195–216, 271–275.

2. E. G. Boring, "Intelligence as the Tests Test It," *New Republic,* June 6, 1923, 35–37.

3. A. Binet and T. Simon, *The Development of Intelligence in Children,* trans. E. S. Kite (Baltimore, Md.: Williams & Wilkins, 1916); D. A. Wechsler, *The Measurement of Adult Intelligence* (Baltimore, Md.: Williams & Wilkins, 1939).

4. F. Galton, *Inquiry into Human Faculty and Its Development* (London: Macmillan, 1883).

5. M. C. Frey and D. K. Detterman, "Scholastic Assessment or *g?* The Relationship between the Scholastic Assessment Test and General Cognitive Ability," *Psychological Science* 15 (2004): 373–378.

6. C. Spearman, *The Abilities of Man* (New York: Macmillan, 1927).

7. A. R. Jensen, *The g Factor* (Westport, Conn.: Praeger, 1998).

8. L. L. Thurstone, *Primary Mental Abilities* (Chicago: University of Chicago Press, 1938).

9. R. B. Cattell, *Abilities: Their Structure, Growth, and Action* (Boston: Houghton Mifflin, 1971); J. B. Carroll, *Human Cognitive Abilities: A Survey of Factor-Analytic Studies* (New York: Cambridge University Press, 1993).

10. C. Spearman, *The Nature of "Intelligence" and the Principles of Cognition* (London: Macmillan, 1923).

11. J. W. Pellegrino and R. Glaser, "Components of Inductive Reasoning," and R. E. Snow, "Aptitude Processes," both in R. E. Snow, P.-A. Federico, and W. E. Montague, eds., *Aptitude, Learning, and Instruction,* vol. 1: *Cognitive Process Analyses of Aptitude* (Hillsdale, N.J.: Lawrence Erlbaum, 1980); R. J. Sternberg, "Components of Human Intelligence," *Cognition* 15 (1983): 1–48; and R. J. Sternberg, *Beyond IQ: A Triarchic Theory of Human Intelligence* (New York: Cambridge University Press, 1985).

12. J. Piaget, *The Psychology of Intelligence* (Totowa, N.J.: Littlefield Adams, 1972).

13. M. Daneman and P. A. Carpenter, "Individual Differences in Working Memory and Reading," *Journal of Verbal Learning and Verbal Behavior* 19 (1980): 450–466; R. W. Engle, S. W. Tuholski, J. E. Laughlin, and A. R. A. Conway, "Working Memory, Short-term Memory and General Fluid Intelligence: A Latent Variable Approach," *Journal of Experimental Psychology: General* 128, no. 3 (1999): 309–331;

D. Z. Hambrick, M. J. Kane, and R. Engle, "The Role of Working Memory in Higher-level Cognition: Domain-Specific vs. Domain-General Perspectives," in R. J. Sternberg and J. E. Pretz, eds., *Cognition and Intelligence* (New York: Cambridge University Press, 2005); P. C. Kyllonen, "Is Working Memory Capacity Spearman's *g?*" in I. Dennis and P. Tapsfield, eds., *Human Abilities: Their Nature and Measurement* (Mahwah, N.J.: Erlbaum, 1996), pp. 49–75.

14. R. J. Herrnstein and C. Murray, *The Bell Curve* (New York: Free Press, 1994); Jensen, *The g Factor.*

15. S. Yang and R. J. Sternberg, "Taiwanese Chinese People's Conceptions of Intelligence," *Intelligence* 25 (1997): 21–36.

16. R. J. Sternberg, B. E. Conway, J. L. Ketron, and M. Bernstein, "People's Conceptions of Intelligence," *Journal of Personality and Social Psychology* 41 (1981): 37–55.

17. P. M. Ruzgis and E. L. Grigorenko, "Cultural Meaning Systems, Intelligence and Personality," in R. J. Sternberg and P. Ruzgis, eds., *Personality and Intelligence* (New York: Cambridge University Press, 1994), pp. 248–270.

18. R. Serpell, "Aspects of Intelligence in a Developing Country," *African Social Research* 17 (1974): 576–596.

19. C. M. Super and S. Harkness, "The Developmental Niche: A Conceptualization at the Interface of Child and Culture," *International Journal of Behavioral Development* 9 (1986): 545–569; C. M. Super and S. Harkness, "The Developmental Niche: A Conceptualization at the Interface of Child and Culture," in R. A. Pierce and M. A. Black, eds., *Life-Span Development: A Diversity Reader* (Dubuque, Iowa: Kendall/Hunt, 1993), pp. 61–77.

20. P. Dasen, "The Cross-Cultural Study of Intelligence: Piaget and the Baoule," *International Journal of Psychology* 19 (1984): 407–434. It is difficult to separate linguistic differences from conceptual differences in cross-cultural notions of intelligence. In our own research, we use converging operations in order to achieve some separation. That is, we approach the question in both varied and overlapping ways. So we may ask in one study that people identify aspects of competence; in another study, that they identify competent people; in a third study, that they characterize the meaning of "intelligence," and so forth.

21. E. L. Grigorenko, P. W. Geissler, R. Prince, F. Okatcha, C. Nokes, D. A. Kenny, D. A. Bundy, and R. J. Sternberg, "The Organization of Luo Conceptions of Intelligence: A Study of Implicit Theories in a Kenyan Village," *International Journal of Behavioral Development* 25, no. 4 (2001): 367–378. See also R. J. Sternberg, "Culture and Intelligence," *American Psychologist* 59, no. 5 (2004): 325–338.

22. L. Okagaki and R. J. Sternberg, "Parental Beliefs and Children's School Performance," *Child Development* 64, no. 1 (1993): 36–56.

23. R. J. Sternberg, "The Theory of Successful Intelligence," *Review of General Psychology* 3 (1999): 292–316; R. J. Sternberg, "The Theory of Successful Intelligence," *Interamerican Journal of Psychology* 39, no. 2 (2005): 189–202; R. J. Sternberg, "Wisdom, Intelligence, and Creativity Synthesized," *School Administrator* 66, no. 2 (2009): 10–14; R. J. Sternberg, "Assessment of Gifted Students for Identification Purposes: New Techniques for a New Millennium," in *Learning and Individual Differences* (forthcoming).

24. Sternberg, *Beyond IQ*.

25. M. Polanyi, *The Tacit Dimensions* (Garden City, N.Y.: Doubleday, 1966).

26. R. J. Sternberg, K. Nokes, P. W. Geissler, R. Prince, F. Okatcha, D. A. Bundy, and E. L. Grigorenko, "The Relationship between Academic and Practical Intelligence: A Case Study in Kenya," *Intelligence* 29 (2001): 401–418.

27. E. L. Grigorenko, E. Meier, J. Lipka, G. Mohatt, E. Yanez, and R. J. Sternberg, "Academic and Practical Intelligence: A Case Study of the Yup'ik in Alaska," *Learning and Individual Differences* 14 (2004): 183–207.

28. J. P. Guilford, "The Structure of Intellect," *Psychological Bulletin* 53 (1956): 267–293; L. L. Thurstone, *Primary Mental Abilities* (Chicago: University of Chicago Press, 1938).

29. D. A. Wagner, "Memories of Morocco," *Cognitive Psychology* 10 (1978): 1–18.

30. J. M. Kearins, "Visual Spatial Memory in Australian Aboriginal Children of Desert Regions," *Cognitive Psychology* 13 (1981): 434–460.

31. R. J. Sternberg and W. M. Williams, "Does the Graduate Record Examination Predict Meaningful Success in the Graduate Training of Psychologists? A Case Study," *American Psychologist* 52 (1997): 630–641.

32. R. J. Sternberg and W. M. Williams, *How to Develop Student Creativity* (Alexandria, Va.: Association for Supervision and Curriculum Development, 1996); R. J. Sternberg, L. Jarvin, and E. L. Grigorenko, *Teaching for Intelligence, Creativity, and Wisdom* (Thousand Oaks, Calif.: Corwin, 2009).

33. R. J. Sternberg, *Wisdom, Intelligence, and Creativity Synthesized* (New York: Cambridge University Press, 2003); R. J. Sternberg, A. Reznitskaya, and L. Jarvin, "Teaching for Wisdom: What Matters Is

Not Just What Students Know, But How They Use It," *London Review of Education* 5, no. 2 (2007): 143–158.

34. R. J. Sternberg, "A Balance Theory of Wisdom," *Review of General Psychology* 2 (1998): 347–365.

35. B. Latané and J. M. Darley, *Unresponsive Bystander: Why Doesn't He Help?* (Englewood Cliffs, N.J.: Prentice-Hall, 1970).

36. R. J. Sternberg, "Reflections on Ethical Leadership," in D. Ambrose and T. L. Cross, eds., *Morality, Ethics, and Gifted Minds* (New York: Springer, 2009), pp. 19–28.

37. T. Atlas, "The Cost of Corruption," *U.S. News and World Report*, June 9, 2008, pp. 8–9.

38. S. McClellan, *What Happened: Inside the Bush White House and Washington's Culture of Deception* (New York: PublicAffairs, 2008).

39. "Senator Faces List of Assault Allegations," http://www.boston.com/news/local/massachusetts/articles/2008/06/05/senator_faces_list_of_assault_allegations/, 2008 (retrieved June 5, 2008).

40. R. J. Sternberg and E. L. Grigorenko, "Practical Intelligence and Its Development," in R. Bar-On and J. D. A. Parker, eds., *The Handbook of Emotional Intelligence* (San Francisco: Jossey-Bass, 2000), pp. 215–243.

41. "Person of the Week: Enron Whistleblower Sherron Watkins," http://www.time.com/time/pow/article/0,8599,194927,00.html, 2002 (retrieved June 5, 2008)

42. R. J. Sternberg and K. Sternberg, *The Nature of Hate* (New York: Cambridge University Press, 2008).

43. P. Gourevitch, *We Wish to Inform You That Tomorrow We Will Be Killed with Our Families: Stories from Rwanda* (New York: Farrar, Straus & Giroux, 1998).

44. S. Totten, W. S. Parsons, and I. W. Charny, eds., *Century of Genocide: Critical Essays and Eyewitness Accounts,* 2d ed. (New York: Taylor & Francis, 2004).

45. P. Jonsson, "Governor Sanford Facing Impeachment Whispers Again," http://features.csmonitor.com/politics/2009/08/11/governor-sanford-facing-impeachment-whispers-again/, 2009 (retrieved August 15, 2009).

46. H. Gardner, "Are There Additional Intelligences? The Case for Naturalist, Spiritual, and Existential Intelligences," in J. Kane, ed., *Education, Information, and Transformation* (Upper Saddle River, N.J.: Prentice Hall, 1999), pp. 111–131.

47. R. Coles, *The Moral Intelligence of Children: How to Raise a Moral Child* (New York: Plume, 1998).

48. L. Kohlberg, *The Psychology of Moral Development: The Nature and Validity of Moral Stages* (New York: HarperCollins, 1984).

49. R. J. Sternberg, "The WICS Approach to Leadership: Stories of Leadership and the Structures and Processes That Support Them," *Leadership Quarterly* 19, no. 3 (2008): 360–371.

50. A. Bandura, "Moral Disengagement in the Perpetration of Inhumanities," *Personality and Social Psychology Review* 3 (1999): 193–209.

51. "Timeline of the Tyco International Scandal," http://www.usatoday.com/money/industries/manufacturing/2005-06-17-tyco-timeline_x.htm, 2005 (retrieved June 5, 2008).

52. H. Gardner, *Frames of Mind: The Theory of Multiple Intelligences* (New York: Basic Books, 1983).

53. "Spitzer Is Linked to Prostitution Ring," http://www.nytimes.com/2008/03/10/nyregion/10cnd-spitzer.html?_r=1&oref=slogin, 2008 (retrieved June 5, 2008).

54. Research by Terezhina Nuñes and others on Brazilian street children shows, for example, that they risk death if they cannot form a successful street business. See T. Nuñes, "Street Intelligence," in R. J. Sternberg, ed., *Encyclopedia of Human Intelligence,* vol. 2 (New York: Macmillan, 1994), pp. 1045–1049.

5. ASSESSING HIDDEN TALENTS

1. R. J. Sternberg, M. Ferrari, P. R. Clinkenbeard, and E. L. Grigorenko, "Identification, Instruction, and Assessment of Gifted Children: A Construct Validation of a Triarchic Model," *Gifted Child Quarterly* 40 (1996): 129–137.

2. R. J. Sternberg, B. Torff, and E. L. Grigorenko, "Teaching Triarchically Improves School Achievement," *Journal of Educational Psychology* 90 (1998): 374–384; E. L. Grigorenko, L. Jarvin, and R. J. Sternberg, "School-based Tests of the Triarchic Theory of Intelligence: Three Settings, Three Samples, Three Syllabi," *Contemporary Educational Psychology* 27 (2002): 167–208; R. J. Sternberg, E. L. Grigorenko, and L.-F. Zhang, "Styles of Learning and Thinking Matter in Instruction and Assessment," *Perspectives on Psychological Science* 3, no. 6 (2008): 486–506.

3. R. J. Sternberg and the Rainbow Project Collaborators, "Augmenting the SAT through Assessments of Analytical, Practical, and Creative Skills," in W. Camara and E. Kimmel, eds., *Choosing Students: Higher Education Admission Tools for the Twenty-first Century* (Mahwah, N.J.: Lawrence Erlbaum, 2005), pp. 159–176; R. J. Sternberg and the Rainbow Project Collaborators, "The Rainbow Project:

Enhancing the SAT through Assessments of Analytical, Practical and Creative Skills," *Intelligence* 34, no. 4 (2006): 321–350.

4. R. J. Sternberg, "Theory-based Testing of Intellectual Abilities: Rationale for the Triarchic Abilities Test," in H. Rowe, ed., *Intelligence: Reconceptualization and Measurement* (Hillsdale, N.J.: Lawrence Erlbaum, 1991), pp. 183–202; R. J. Sternberg, J. L. Castejón, M. D. Prieto, J. Hautamäki, and E. L. Grigorenko, "Confirmatory Factor Analysis of the Sternberg Triarchic Abilities Test in Three International Samples: An Empirical Test of the Triarchic Theory of Intelligence," *European Journal of Psychological Assessment* 17, no. 1 (2001): 1–16.

5. R. J. Sternberg and T. I. Lubart, *Defying the Crowd: Cultivating Creativity in a Culture of Conformity* (New York: Free Press, 1995); R. J. Sternberg and T. I. Lubart, "Investing in Creativity," *American Psychologist* 51, no. 7 (1996): 677–688.

6. R. J. Sternberg, G. B. Forsythe, J. Hedlund, J. Horvath, S. Snook, W. M. Williams, R. K. Wagner, and E. L. Grigorenko, *Practical Intelligence in Everyday Life* (New York: Cambridge University Press, 2000).

7. J. J. McArdle and F. Hamagami, "Modeling Incomplete Longitudinal and Cross-Sectional Data Using Latent Growth Structural Models," *Experimental Aging Research* 18, no. 3 (1992): 145–166.

8. R. J. Sternberg, the Rainbow Project Collaborators, and University of Michigan Business School Project Collaborators, "Theory-Based University Admissions Testing for a New Millennium," *Educational Psychologist* 39, no. 3 (2004): 185–198; J. Hedlund, J. M. Wilt, K. R. Nebel, S. J. Ashford, and R. J. Sternberg, "Assessing Practical Intelligence in Business School Admissions: A Supplement to the Graduate Management Admissions Test," *Learning and Individual Differences* 16 (2006): 101–127.

9. S. E. Stemler, E. L. Grigorenko, L. Jarvin, and R. J. Sternberg, "Using the Theory of Successful Intelligence as a Basis for Augmenting AP Exams in Psychology and Statistics," *Contemporary Educational Psychology* 31, no. 2 (2006): 344–376; S. E. Stemler, R. J. Sternberg, E. L. Grigorenko, L. Jarvin, and D. K. Sharpes, "Using the Theory of Successful Intelligence as a Framework for Developing Assessments in AP Physics," *Contemporary Educational Psychology* 34 (2009): 195–209.

10. H. Chart, E. L. Grigorenko, and R. J. Sternberg, "Identification: The Aurora Battery," in J. A. Plucker and C. M. Callahan, eds., *Critical Issues and Practices in Gifted Education* (Waco, Tex.: Prufrock, 2008), pp. 281–301.

11. R. J. Sternberg, "Finding Students Who Are Wise, Practical, and Creative," *Chronicle of Higher Education* 53, no. 44 (2007): B11; R. J.

Sternberg, "Enhancing Academic Excellence and Diversity," in B. Lauren, ed., *The College Admissions Officer's Guide* (Washington, D.C.: American Association of Collegiate Registrars and Admissions Officers, 2008), pp. 387–397; R. J. Sternberg, "The Rainbow and Kaleidoscope Projects: A New Psychological Approach to Undergraduate Admissions," *European Psychologist* 14, no. 4 (2009): 279–287; R. J. Sternberg, C. R. Bonney, L. Gabora, L. Jarvin, T. M. Karelitz, and L. Coffin, *Broadening the Spectrum of Undergraduate Admissions* (manuscript submitted for publication, 2009); R. J. Sternberg and L. A. Coffin, "Kaleidoscope: Admitting and Developing 'New Leaders for a Changing World,'" *New England Journal of Higher Education* (Winter 2010): 12–13.

12. R. J. Sternberg, "A Decision Rule to Facilitate the Undergraduate Admissions Process," *College and University* 48 (1972): 48–53.

13. J. Hedlund, J. M. Wilt, K. R. Nebel, S. J. Ashford, and R. J. Sternberg, "Assessing Practical Intelligence in Business School Admissions: A Supplement to the Graduate Management Admissions Test," *Learning and Individual Differences* 16 (2006): 101–127.

14. Stemler, Grigorenko, Jarvin, and Sternberg, "Using the Theory of Successful Intelligence as a Basis for Augmenting AP Exams in Psychology and Statistics."

6. ENCOURAGING CREATIVITY, PRACTICAL INTELLIGENCE, AND WISDOM

1. R. J. Sternberg, "Principles of Teaching for Successful Intelligence," *Educational Psychologist* 33 (1998): 65–72; R. J. Sternberg, "Raising the Achievement of All Students: Teaching for Successful Intelligence," *Educational Psychology Review* 14 (2002): 383–393.

2. R. J. Sternberg, *Intelligence Applied: Understanding and Increasing Your Intellectual Skills* (San Diego, Calif.: Harcourt Brace Jovanovich, 1986); R. J. Sternberg, J. C. Kaufman, and E. L. Grigorenko, *Applied Intelligence* (New York: Cambridge University Press, 2008).

3. R. J. Sternberg and E. L. Grigorenko, *Teaching for Successful Intelligence,* 2d ed. (Thousand Oaks, Calif.: Corwin Press, 2007).

4. R. J. Sternberg, E. L. Grigorenko, M. Ferrari, and P. Clinkenbeard, "A Triarchic Analysis of an Aptitude-Treatment Interaction," *European Journal of Psychological Assessment* 15, no. 1 (1999): 1–11.

5. R. J. Sternberg, B. Torff, and E. L. Grigorenko, "Teaching for Successful Intelligence Raises School Achievement," *Phi Delta Kappan* 79 (1998): 667–669; R. J. Sternberg, B. Torff, and E. L. Grigorenko,

"Teaching Triarchically Improves School Achievement," *Journal of Educational Psychology* 90 (1998): 374–384.

6. E. L. Grigorenko, L. Jarvin, and R. J. Sternberg, "School-based Tests of the Triarchic Theory of Intelligence: Three Settings, Three Samples, Three Syllabi," *Contemporary Educational Psychology* 27 (2002): 167–208.

7. R. J. Sternberg, "Reflections on Ethical Leadership," in D. Ambrose and T. L. Cross, eds., *Morality, Ethics, and Gifted Minds* (New York: Springer, 2009).

8. R. J. Sternberg and T. I. Lubart, "An Investment Theory of Creativity and Its Development," *Human Development* 34, no. 1 (1991): 1–31.

9. J. Garcia and R. A. Koelling, "The Relation of Cue to Consequence in Avoidance Learning," *Psychonomic Science* 4 (1966): 123–124.

10. R. J. Sternberg and W. M. Williams, "Teaching for Creativity: Two Dozen Tips," in R. D. Small and A. P. Thomas, eds., *Plain Talk about Education* (Covington, La.: Center for Development and Learning, 2001), pp. 153–165; R. J. Sternberg, "Teaching for Creativity," in R. A. Beghetto and J. C. Kaufman, eds., *Nurturing Creativity in the Classroom* (New York: Cambridge University Press, 2010).

11. R. J. Sternberg, "Allowing for Thinking Styles," *Educational Leadership* 52, no. 3 (1994): 36–40; R. J. Sternberg, *Thinking Styles* (New York: Cambridge University Press, 1997); L.-F. Zhang and R. J. Sternberg, *The Nature of Intellectual Styles* (Mahwah, N.J.: Lawrence Erlbaum, 2006).

12. P. A. Frensch and R. J. Sternberg, "Expertise and Intelligent Thinking: When Is It Worse to Know Better?" in R. J. Sternberg, ed., *Advances in the Psychology of Human Intelligence*, vol. 5 (Hillsdale, N.J.: Lawrence Erlbaum, 1989), pp. 157–188.

13. R. J. Sternberg, "Intelligence and Nonentrenchment," *Journal of Educational Psychology* 73 (1981): 1–16; R. J. Sternberg, "Natural, Unnatural, and Supernatural Concepts," *Cognitive Psychology* 14 (1982): 451–488; S. J. Tetewsky and R. J. Sternberg, "Conceptual and Lexical Determinants of Nonentrenched Thinking," *Journal of Memory and Language* 25 (1986): 202–225.

14. F. Barron, "Putting Creativity to Work," in R. J. Sternberg, ed., *The Nature of Creativity* (New York: Cambridge University Press, 1988), pp. 76–98.

15. A. Bandura, *Self-Efficacy: The Exercise of Control* (New York: Freeman, 1996).

16. W. Mischel, Y. Shoda, and M. L. Rodriguez, "Delay of Gratification in Children," *Science* 244 (1989): 933–938.

17. T. M. Amabile, *The Context of Creativity* (Boulder, Colo.: Westview, 1996).

18. T. M. Amabile, "The Social Psychology of Creativity: A Consensual Assessment Technique," *Journal of Personality and Social Psychology* 43 (1982): 997–1013.

19. R. J. Sternberg, "How Wise Is It to Teach for Wisdom? A Reply to Five Critiques," *Educational Psychologist* 36, no. 4 (2001): 269–272.

20. L. Kohlberg, "The Psychology of Moral Development: The Nature and Validity of Moral Stages," in Kohlberg, *Essays on Moral Development*, vol. 2 (New York: Harper & Row, 1984); C. Gilligan, *In a Different Voice: Psychological Theory and Women's Development* (Cambridge, Mass.: Harvard University Press, 1982).

21. G. W. F. Hegel, *The Phenomenology of Mind*, trans. J. B. Baillie, 2d ed. (1807; London: Allen & Unwin, 1931).

7. IMPLICATIONS FOR STUDENTS, COLLEGES, AND SOCIETY

1. F. Rich, "The Brightest Are Not Always the Best," http://www.nytimes.com/2008/12/07/opinion/07rich.html?_r=1&scp=2&sq=frank%20rich&st=cse, 2008 (retrieved December 7, 2008); D. Halberstam, *The Best and the Brightest* (New York: Ballantine, 1993). See also G. M. Goldstein, *Lessons in Disaster: McGeorge Bundy and the Path to War in Vietnam* (New York: Henry Holt, 2008).

2. J. Kantor and J. C. Hernandez, "A Harvard Lightning Rod Finds Path to Renewal," http://www.nytimes.com/2008/12/07/us/politics/07summers.html?scp=1&sq=larry%20summers&st=cse, 2008 (retrieved December 7, 2008).

3. D. B. Henriques, "Madoff Scheme Kept Rippling Outward, across Borders," http://www.nytimes.com/2008/12/20/business/20madoff.html?_r=1&scp=2&sq=madoff&st=cse, 2008 (retrieved December 20, 2008).

4. H. Gardner, *Multiple Intelligences: New Horizons in Theory and Practice* (New York: Basic Books, 2006); J. R. Renzulli and S. M. Reis, eds., *Identification of Students for Gifted and Talented Programs* (Thousand Oaks, Calif.: Corwin, 2004); S. J. Ceci, *On Intelligence: More or Less* (Cambridge, Mass.: Harvard University Press, 1996).

INDEX

Abilities, viii, x, 6, 30–33, 36, 80, 178. *See also* Skills
Ability tests, 16, 30, 32
Abriola, Linda, 118
Abstract-reasoning-based abilities, 80, 82
Academic success, and test scores, 18, 21, 25, 33, 44
Accountability, 19, 33
Achievement, assessment of, 132–133
Achievement tests, 24, 27, 31
ACT English test, 43
ACT mathematics test, 43
ACT reading test, 43–44
ACT science reasoning test, 44
ACT tests/scores, 2, 4, 13, 173–174; and college application, 41, 43–47; and intelligence, 72, 83; and Rainbow Project, 110, 115, 118; and Kaleidoscope Project, 118–119, 121–122
ACT writing test, 44
Admissions, college, ix–x, 1–3, 33–34; problems concerning, 3–5; valuing additional skills,
5–6; need for change, 6–12; reasons for few changes to date, 12–27; as closed system, 27–31; and broader understanding of intelligence, 31–33; and instruction, 134–137
Admissions officers, 6, 12–14, 18, 28, 120, 129; and college applications, 37, 39–41, 44–45, 47, 51–52
Admissions practices, alternative: affirmative action, 58–62; formulaic admissions, 62–63; lottery-based, 63; open admissions, 63–66; geographically restricted admissions, 66–68; flexible admissions, 68–70
Admissions testing, viii–ix, 33–34; lack of competition, 3, 5; for all skills, 4, 6, 11–12; and socioeconomic status, 7–11, 26–27; skewed, 10; preparation for, 12, 46; precision of measurement, 12–13; attractiveness of successful test takers, 13–17; dangers in ignoring scores,